T0278376

JAPANESE
in
WYOMING

UNION PACIFIC'S FORGOTTEN LABOR FORCE

DANIEL JOHN LYON

THE
History
PRESS

Published by The History Press
Charleston, SC
www.historypress.com

First published 2023

Manufactured in the United States

ISBN 9781467155120

Library of Congress Control Number: 2023938425

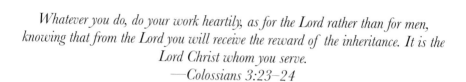

Whatever you do, do your work heartily, as for the Lord rather than for men, knowing that from the Lord you will receive the reward of the inheritance. It is the Lord Christ whom you serve.
—Colossians 3:23–24

To my mom, who encouraged me to write and to embrace my Japanese heritage. And to my friend Jim Allison. Thank you for asking a question about Cheyenne's Japanese community that I couldn't answer. You two are the reason I wrote this book.

CONTENTS

PREFACE

My intention wasn't to write a book about Japanese immigration in Wyoming. But I'm glad I did. This book captures an important but forgotten chapter of Wyoming's history of the unwanted immigrants who helped shape and build the state and Union Pacific's economy during a period of realignment and construction.

The goal of this book is to honor the forgotten generation of Japanese controversially hired by the Union Pacific at the turn of the twentieth century. In *Japanese in Wyoming: Union Pacific's Forgotten Labor Force*, I try to give a general idea of where Japan town was in each county. Then, I share stories of how the Japanese lived, died and integrated into their adopted state. Finally, I explain how Wyoming State laws and national laws both legally discriminated against and benefited Japanese immigrants.

This book doesn't cover the social injustice and incarceration of people of Japanese heritage at Heart Mountain because Wyoming's Japanese population was not affected by Executive Order 9066.

ACKNOWLEDGEMENTS

A special thanks to Jim Allison, a high school friend and the former collection supervisor for the Wyoming State Museum, for his inspiration in researching the topic; to Suzi Taylor and Robin Everett at the Wyoming State Archives for their archival expertise; to Jane Nelson of the Albany County Historical Society and Dakota Russell, the former executive director of Heart Mountain Interpretive Center, for help in establishing contacts; to Don Aoki, Stacie Kageyama, Kathryn Mlsna, Aileen Tanimoto and Russ Endo for sharing family stories and family photos; to Jennifer Messer at the Rock Springs Historical Museum and Caitlyn Heusser of the Windsor History Museum for their assistance; and to the Utah State Historical Society for access to its Japanese American Oral History Program. To Steve Fiscor, editor and publisher of *Coal Age Magazine*, thank you for permission to reprint a photo from *Coal Age*'s 1916 edition.

INTRODUCTION

J apanese labor was a cheaper labor source for the Union Pacific because they worked for "coolie" wages. As a result, Wyoming labor unions accused Japanese immigrants of taking "white man" jobs. But how can an immigrant take a job away if the job isn't wanted?

In the early 1900s, the company upgraded its infrastructure in the Wyoming Division. This $5 million project entailed double-tracking existing lines, building cutoffs to shorten the distance between stations, reducing steep grades, building bridges and boring through solid granite to build tunnels. Union Pacific advertised for help, but only some men applied. The company was in receivership and made some economic concessions by cutting section laborer wages. What incentive did the average American have to apply for a backbreaking job with the railroad when salespeople lived at the top of the food chain?

Union Pacific had no other recourse than to hire Japanese immigrants at unskilled laborer wages. Newspapers joined the anti-Japanese bandwagon and vilified the Japanese. The media recycled yellow peril rhetoric, printed sensational headlines and ran poorly fact-checked articles portraying the Japanese as evil labor.

The Japanese, however, were loyal to Wyoming. The Japanese community gave generously of their meager earnings to support Liberty Bond drives and Red Cross subscriptions. The Japanese sponsored local Fourth of July fireworks shows and even volunteered for the draft. In return, the Japanese community experienced prejudice and violence. The good citizens of

Evanston made a threat to blow them up. The residents of Rawlins proudly ran the Japanese out of town. And boys in Laramie waged a three-day riot against the Japanese. Wyoming laws also discriminated against Asians. For example, it was a felony for a Japanese person to marry a white woman.

Yet despite prejudice and their humble existence, the Japanese laid down roots in their adopted state of Wyoming.

Meet the Japanese in Wyoming: Union Pacific's forgotten labor force.

PART I

CAN OF WORMS

Union Pacific and its subsidiaries hired Japanese immigrants on both sides of the twentieth century. Their arrival in 1892 in the small town of Granger merited only a one-line story. However, the hatred for the "little brown men" from the Flowery Kingdom who traveled the ocean blue to take "white man" jobs grew, and it showed on the 1900 census. In Granger, Wyoming, the census taker listed Japanese section workers as numbers. Even dogs had names. Newspapers also imitated this practice. For example,

Overland Limited train crossing bridge. The first Japanese in Wyoming worked for the Oregon Short Line Railway at Granger in 1892. Their presence merited one line in the newspaper. *Wyoming State Archives.*

It was common practice to marginalize the Japanese by giving them numbers instead of names. *United States Census, 1900, Sweetwater County, Granger.*

when a Japanese laborer assaulted his foreman in 1902, the *Cheyenne Daily Leader* identified him as Number 27.[1]

The perceived problem of Japanese immigrant labor is one created by the United States. Back in 1853, Commodore Matthew Perry threatened to blow up the capital city of Edo if the Japanese didn't open its borders to Western influence and trade. Little did America know just how big a can of worms it opened with such a demand. Sometimes you have to be careful about what you wish.

Opening Japan's borders allowed Japanese subjects to immigrate to the sugarcane fields of Hawai'i and the mainland's West Coast and eventually to the Intermountain West states and Wyoming to work for Union Pacific. But unfortunately, newspapers of America conditioned readers to believe the huddled masses who came to America were secretly the Japanese army plotting a takeover of America.

CHAPTER 1

ALL JAPANESE ARE SPIES

The idea that all Japanese immigrants were spies was popularized around the time of the Japanese-Russo War. In 1908, a Washington special report said, "Almost the entire Japanese secret service is operating in America and gathering information of every nature." Newspapers such as the *Copper Mountain Miner* postulated that the "Japs" would invade America. And what of America's secret source? He was a prominent Russian who "did his best to warn America against the wiles of the Jap."[2]

Was this witness credible, or was this another ploy by corporate newspapers to sell more subscriptions by reporting fake news or news with a hint of truth? Newspapers made it easy to believe Union Pacific hired secret members of the Japanese army as section workers in its Wyoming Division. For example, in October 1904, the *Wyoming Tribune* reported a mass recall of "Japs" employed in Union Pacific's Wyoming Division for service in the First and Second Army Reserve during the Japanese-Russo War. The anonymous reporter estimated the call to arms affected "600 Japs in Utah, [and] about 400 in Wyoming and probably 100 in Colorado." There were also "many thousands" of Japanese people on the Pacific coast affected.[3] Three weeks later, the *Tribune* said Cheyenne's Japanese labor agent, George Wakimoto, informed them that the number of Japanese section men deployed back to Japan was closer to six.[4]

Publishing tycoon William Randolph Hearst was an influential man and the father of yellow journalism. His use of tabloid-style headlines and exaggerated human-interest stories influenced mainstream public opinion against the Japanese who came to Wyoming to achieve their American Dream of prosperity. This poison-pen type of reporting recycled yellow peril rhetoric once used to describe the Chinese who came to America in search of a better life, just as the other immigrant refugees who came before them.

And like the Chinese, the Japanese quickly discovered that America did not want their huddled masses teeming on its shores, because the Japanese were the latest existential threat to the Western world, and "they" did not look like the average American or white European immigrant. Wyoming newspapers warned about the new invasion of Asiatic breaching its borders with headlines that screamed, "The Japs Are Coming"[5] and "Don't Like Japs."[6] This journalistic style often sparked violence against the Asian community. When the Japanese arrived in the cowboy state in the early 1900s, they received a big Wyoming Welcome. The citizens of Evanston tried to blow them up. Over the years, Rawlins chased them out of town, and Laramie rioted against them.

As a result of what they were led to think, Americans believed the Chinese Exclusion Act should also include the Japanese for fear "they" would invade and take over America. This fear led to the creation of the Asian Exclusion League.

In 1908, anti-Japanese sentiment reached a fevered pitch, and newspapers such as the *Cheyenne Daily Leader* earnestly promoted the "all Japanese immigrants are spies" conspiracy theory. There were reports of Japanese spies at Fort D.A. Russell and spies watching fifteen thousand military troops perform maneuvers outside Laramie. The *Cheyenne Daily Leader* also reported that a trio of Japanese spies posed as laborers and made extensive observations at Fort Russell in February 1908. The "spies" allegedly took photographs and made notes of the location of the post and its "defenses."[7] I am very familiar with the frontier army post named after Brigadier General David Allen Russell. I worked for the base museum for five years. There is nothing to see on that part of the post except open prairie and antelopes. Fort D.A. Russell was established in 1867 to protect workers during the construction of the Transcontinental Railroad. The Thirtieth Infantry first garrisoned at the post, and Fort Russell became a brigade-sized post in 1906, but FDAR had no fortifications, so it was an open post. Cheyenne citizens often came to the post and watched the soldiers drill and listened to the military band. The U.S. Army also employed two Japanese men at the post. One was a domestic servant for an officer, and the other was the cook for the artillery.

Evidence shows that Japanese laborers may have been part of a crew that surveyed Fort D.A. Russell. They, however, weren't spies—they worked as laborers for a Burlington Railroad survey crew. The railway wanted to build a spur from Cheyenne to Fort D.A. Russell around May 1908. The proposed line would skirt Lake Minnehaha in east Cheyenne, pass a draw east of the city cemetery, skirt the four lakes north of the capitol building and then run directly across the military reservation to Laramie.[8]

The following month, the *Cheyenne Daily Leader* carried a news story that said that Japan wanted Yankee spies to locate mines and gather descriptions of the San Francisco and San Diego Harbors and the Puget Sound fortifications. The agent allegedly offered to pay a former Twenty-First Infantry troop $150 monthly for his service.[9] The soldier, however, opted to enlist in the army and earn $13 monthly as a private. Finally, in August 1908, the *Cheyenne Daily Leader* said Japanese spies watched military maneuvers at Fort D.A. Russell Target and Maneuver Reservation twenty-two miles outside Laramie. The newspaper speculated the Japanese wanted to "acquire" the secret of the

The Japanese showed patriotism during World War I by volunteering for the draft and supporting war bond drives and Red Cross subscriptions. *Wyoming State Archives.*

Aspen Railroad Tunnel was one of the Union Pacific's critical infrastructures protected by Wyoming National Guardsmen during World War I. *Wyoming State Archives.*

machine gun used by two companies of the Eighth Cavalry. The alleged spy was discovered by an officer with field glasses watching a skirmish between a Utah battery called the "Jackass" battery and the regular infantry. The officer spied a "figure of a man perched on a pinnacle of rock, watching the troops at work. He had glasses and made frequent notes."

The *Cheyenne Daily Leader* said two soldiers were detailed to capture the man, but he disappeared. According to the *Leader*, the Japanese spy resurfaced later at the home of a woman living three miles from the Fort D.A. Russell Artillery and Maneuver Reservation, dressed as a laborer. The Japanese man told the homeowner he worked for the Union Pacific and had become ill and wanted a place to rest. The woman became suspicious of his story and refused to take him in, which "greatly disappointed" the man.[10]

Newspapers were not the only ones to vilify the Japanese. Leading universities, theater productions and novels entertained the American public with tales about the evil Japanese. In his 1908 book *Banzai!*, author Ferdinand Heinrich Grautoff expanded on this theme that all Japanese are spies. The premise of the book was that the Asian Exclusion League and unionized labor feared that a workforce that was a secret Japanese army would infiltrate the railroad and conquer the Intermountain West and West Coast. In the novel, a secret Japanese army posing as section workers on the Oregon Short Line Rail Road establishes an artillery battery and captures communication lines from Granger, Wyoming, to the West Coast. Within forty-eight hours, the Japanese flag flies over Wyoming and the western United States. There was a sprinkle of truth in this novel, because the Oregon Short Line did employ Japanese section workers in 1892. And the Japanese flag did fly over Cheyenne once.[11] But the act wasn't sinister. The Japanese flag flew to commemorate the death of the emperor. The Japanese flag displayed at the Japanese Supply Company also respectfully flew underneath the American flag.

The Japanese weren't spies. They came to Wyoming to work for Union Pacific so they could achieve their share of the American Dream of prosperity. They were loyal to their adopted state. Moreover, the Japanese supported Wyoming war efforts by purchasing Liberty Bond and Red Cross subscriptions. Many Japanese people living in Wyoming even volunteered for the draft during World War I. The Japanese also volunteered to serve during World War II despite the imprisonment of Japanese Americans at the relocation authority camps such as Heart Mountain in northern Wyoming.

COMING TO AMERICA

Japanese immigrant labor was a hot-button topic in the early twentieth century. But Union Pacific had the final say on whether they should stay or go.

The greatest criticism of import Japanese labor came from labor unions and newspapers that argued that Japanese immigrants took "white man" jobs. However, when Union Pacific advertised for help in local papers, few white men applied. Union Pacific had little recourse but to hire Japanese laborers provided by Japanese contracting agents to fill the void. Hyoza Harry Kumagai was one of the Japanese who came to America to work for Union Pacific in the coal mines of Rock Springs in the early 1900s. When Commodore Perry opened the ports of Japan, it ended 265 years of Sakoku, a Japanese closed-border policy. Japan now allowed its citizens to immigrate outside the country for work. Hyoza said his father, Isokichi, and brother left Japan and toiled in the sugarcane fields of Hawai'i for

JAPANESE IN WYOMING

one dollar a day. Hyoza's mother supported the family by making brooms out of palm tree leaves and branches. She also made rope and twine from pine leaves and stems. Whenever she could make three hundred feet of rope, she sold it to the fishermen for eleven cents. Hyoza dropped out of school to help with the family finances. He delivered newspapers daily from Yamakita to Fukuro, a round trip of twenty-five miles. He earned six cents a day from his route. With his mother's income, seventeen cents made a comfortable living for five people.[12]

Leaving Japan for work was a faster path to prosperity for Hyoza and many other Japanese people. Japanese labor contractors on both sides of the Pacific Ocean lured prospective clients with promises of big paydays and transportation. The business of Japanese contract labor was so profitable that a labor agent in Tacoma, Washington, was said to have made $400 a month in commissions after paying his Japanese employees ninety cents a day.

Shintaro Takaki, a Japanese restaurant owner in Oregon, was the man who originally introduced Japanese labor to Wyoming. Takaki met the men at his restaurant and learned that an unscrupulous labor agent had hired the men for nonexistent railroad jobs in Oregon. He cared for the men and used his connections to find legitimate work for them in exchange for a small commission. The good Samaritan contacted his friend Tadashichi Tanaka (some sources say Chushichi Tanaka) for help finding the men jobs on the Oregon Short Line. Tanaka is a good example of how profitable it was to hire Japanese immigrant labor. Tanaka was a railroad subcontractor who subcontracted from a Chinese subcontractor, who subcontracted from W.H. Remington, a white American, who contracted for the Oregon Short Line. Tanaka later cut out the Chinese middleman and worked directly for Remington out of an office in Nampa, Idaho. By September 1892, he had five hundred workers employed on the Oregon Short Line, including the forty Japanese laborers between Oregon and the Granger terminal.

The Japanese labor agents' employment system operated similarly to the Italian padrones. The padrone system was a brokering program that addressed a growing need for immigrant labor. The system arranged transportation from the homeland; housed the immigrants; provided the immigrants' jobs, interpretation services and supplies; and handled the payroll. Under the Japanese "boss system," there were tier-level bosses who profited handsomely from immigrant sweat equity.

While the "boss system" provided a much-needed service to facilitate Japanese immigrant employment in industry, it was also an abusive system

22

that often didn't deliver on pay promises. Labor agents often induced the Japanese with a promise of higher wages, but because of "extenuating circumstances," immigrants accepted lower wages. And in some cases, there were no payouts on payday. For example, in Thermopolis, there were reports that "there had been an awful riot among the Japs working on one of the contracts of the canyon work, and that over twenty men had been killed."[13]

However, the reports of Japanese deaths were greatly exaggerated, and the writer of the *Big Horn County Rustler* expressed his disappointment: "Thus was another big newspaper story spoiled." The *Rustler* said, "The trouble had arisen on the account of the financial embarrassment of the Jap contractor who had charge of a part of the work. The agent was unable to pay his men, and they became 'crazed' and commenced rioting. Fortunately, the contractor managed to barricade himself from the angry men; the Japanese rioters held him at bay but they surrendered themselves to local authorities when they arrived to quell the riot."

Even Japanese-born agents such as Tanaka took advantage of their fellow Japanese. Tanaka embezzled money from his compatriots and lived riotously in Utah before relinquishing his contract to furnish Japanese labor to the Oregon Short Line. Narita Yasuteru succeeded Tanaka in 1894. Kumamoto Hifumi held the labor contract between 1895 and 1897. Hajime Nishiyama, a Salt Lake City contracting agent, is also mentioned as a source of Japanese contract labor.

R. Kondo, a representative for the Ashio copper mines in Japan, addressed the growing concern Americans had about Japanese immigrant labor at a meeting of the Western Federation of Miners and the Western Labor Union in Denver, Colorado, in May 1900.

Kondo said emigration agents and steamship companies profited from the steady stream of Japanese immigrating for work to the United States. Because of the scarcity of laborers, industries such as Union Pacific were anxious to find a new labor source. After exhausting the European labor market, agents lured the Japanese with promises of $1.50 a day. Little did the Japanese immigrants realize that surcharges for services would eat up most of their promised pay. Kondo explained the economic woes the average Japanese worker faced in Japan. Earning $1 a day was double the wages of the common laborer in Japan. To provide a better life for themselves and their families, the Japanese sought employment outside the country. They registered with contracting agents and boarded ships with names as the *Tacoma Maru* and the SS *Goodwin*, which sailed from Kobe, Nagasaki and Yokohama ports. These agents overcharged immigrants for the trans-Pacific passage. Agents charged fifty-six yen for a sixteen-yen ticket, and they packed the immigrants in the cargo hold like sardines for a two-week journey. The agents had the Japanese immigrants over a barrel. The immigrants had little recourse but to pay the exorbitant fee and sail to America because they sold their possessions or they had to save face because they borrowed money from relatives to finance their travel. When they disembarked at one of the port cities, immigrants had to show a minimum of $30 to gain entry or risk deportation. Many labor agents circumvented the policy by fronting the money, which then passed from immigrant to immigrant.

Some Japanese immigrants entered the country illegally. They often joined a vessel as crew and then jumped overboard when the ship entered a port city. Other illegal aliens obtained fraudulent passports or crossed illegally at the Canadian or Mexican borders. There are even humorous stories about Japanese immigrants who gained entry into the United States by walking backward on a bridge between the United States and Canada. When American border agents discovered them, they ran for the Canadian border. Agents escorted any apprehended border breacher back to the United States. Illegally crossing the southern border from Mexico was more hazardous because of the extreme heat and the risk of dying from dehydration, sun-related injuries and wild animal encounters.

To combat the influx of Japanese immigrants, the United States passed reforms to curb Japanese immigration. In 1903, the United States passed an alien act that put a head tax on all arriving passengers. In addition, the Immigration Act of 1907 and the gentlemen's agreement between the United States and the Japanese government aimed to stop the emigration of Japanese labor. The Immigration Act of 1907 prohibited Asians from entering the United States through the territory of Hawai'i. Those groups affected by the new restrictions included contract laborers and subversive and presumably immoral groups. The law also doubled the immigration head tax to four dollars per person. The gentlemen's agreement was an informal agreement between the United States and Japan, and its goal was to peacefully resolve a school segregation dispute in California that barred Japanese and Korean students from attending public schools.

In 1924, an immigration act excluded all immigrants from Asia.

CHAPTER 2

UNION PACIFIC LABOR AGENTS

The business of Japanese contract labor was lucrative. Hajime Nishiyama was a contractor who supplied Union Pacific with Japanese labor in southwest Wyoming before the turn of the century. As Union Pacific's demand for labor increased, the company relied on four labor agents: Martin M. O'Malley, George Wakimoto, Ryuun Nishimura and Shinzaburo Ban. O'Malley was born in Missouri in 1859 and worked in Pocatello, Idaho, before transferring to the Wyoming Division. He profited by charging each immigrant ten cents a day commission to handle their affairs.

The *Carbon County Journal* gave this biased assessment of the coming Japanese labor: "The Japs will receive $1.15 per day while the men now employed receive $1.65." They said Union Pacific would make quite a saving by the change, but the gain to the company would be a decided loss to the country, as the men who would be displaced were principally Scandinavians, whom everybody knew to be a good class of citizens—men who readily assimilated with Americans and learned our ways.[14]

O'Malley finished his career in Wyoming as a clerk at the Union Pacific office in Cheyenne and moved back to Pocatello in 1910.[15]

The Wakimoto-Nishimura Company was the largest employer of Japanese contract labor. The company was headquartered in Cheyenne and employed between eight hundred and one thousand contract laborers on the Union Pacific Railroad and in its company-owned mines. In addition, Wakimoto-Nishimura provided interpretation, payroll and human resources for Japanese immigrants in Wyoming, Colorado and Nebraska. The company also built a Japanese hospital with a boardinghouse upstairs at 714 West Fifteenth Street. The hospital was a story-and-a-half structure with a covered porch. It had two wards and a dispensary, and there was one doctor and two nurses on staff.

George Wakimoto was born in Japan in 1859 and immigrated to the United States in 1888. He worked in Los Angeles in 1900 as a Japanese labor contractor for the Santa Fe Railroad. He moved to Cheyenne in 1903 and formed the Wakimoto-Nishimura Company. Ryuun Nishimura, also known as Tatsumo Nishimura, worked as a subcontractor for the Santa Fe Railroad in San Francisco in 1900. He, too, moved to Cheyenne in 1903. In 1907, he returned to Japan and established a branch office in Kobe, Japan.

Shinzaburo Ban was perhaps the most successful and influential Japanese contractor in the western United States. Headquartered in Portland, Oregon, Ban had company offices and stores in Osaka and Tokyo, Japan; Denver, Colorado; Seattle, Washington; Ogden, Utah; and Cheyenne and Sheridan, Wyoming.

He was born in Tokyo and studied English with the American missionary James Hepburn. Ban resigned from his post as a diplomat at the Japanese Consul-General in Honolulu. Instead, he started a Japanese labor contract business, supplying workers to American railroads, mines, farms and the fishing and lumber industries. To help early immigrants understand what was happening in the world, Ban started a Japanese newspaper. His business acumen made him one of the wealthiest Japanese people outside Japan.

Despite his tremendous wealth, Ban was very generous with contract laborers. For example, when federal laws regarding Japanese immigrants became more restrictive, Ban reduced his commission from ten cents a day to five. Hajime Nishiyama and George Wakimoto also took an interest in their compatriots' welfare. Hajime never talked about how much he made, but he had a habit of smoking five-dollar cigars. Nishiyama often gave "anybody hundreds of dollars, or whatever was necessary to tide them over, if they came to him with a sob story."[16] Wakimoto, on the other hand, sponsored Japanese celebrations and is known to have lent money to his charges.

CHAPTER 3

WORKING FOR UNION PACIFIC

U nion Pacific Railroad controversially hired Japanese immigrants as section workers on the railroad or as coal miners because it had trouble attracting help for its $5 million infrastructure upgrade project (this amount in 1900 is more than $171,133,000 in 2022). The infrastructure upgrade required double-tracking existing lines in southern Wyoming; drilling tunnels through solid granite walls; reducing grades; replacing old wooden trestle bridges built during the original railroad construction; and construction of new rail spurs. Union Pacific needed section workers and coal miners to extract the coal that fed hungry steam-driven engines. They used Japanese immigrants for their labor needs. However, people from a country with a red circle on its flag couldn't lay down roots in a square-shaped state because labor unions wanted a more homogenous workforce resembling the pioneers who settled the state.

A reason Union Pacific had difficulty attracting non-Asian laborers was that it was bankrupt. The company fell into hard times in 1893 when the country was amid a financial panic. The court placed the company into receivership when it couldn't generate enough income from transcontinental traffic to pay the interest on its debts. Edward Harriman was the visionary who helped reorganize and rebuild Union Pacific. On January 27, 1894, the Union Pacific receiving board bypassed collective bargaining with unions and filed a lengthy petition with the federal courts in several states to reduce the employees' wages to encourage "certain economics in operations." Five years later, Union Pacific wanted to cut the salaries of the section men by fifteen cents per day. Why work for Union Pacific when salesmen lived at the top of the food chain because of a potential three-figure-a-month income and skilled laborers as "carpenters, bricklayers, and plasters earned almost twice a white man's wage"?

Why work for the railroad when there were better money opportunities elsewhere? How far down the employment labor pool did the Union Pacific have to go to hire someone with the résumé of Skegami Kitichitaro? Skegami was a section laborer in the Cheyenne District in 1910. He labored ten hours a day, six days a week, shoveling prodigious amounts of rock ballast. He moved two-hundred-pound railroad ties and other jobs as assigned. He fit the description of a typical Japanese laborer; he was short and slight in build. On a good day when he didn't have sore muscles and could stand straight, Skegami was more than a foot and a half taller than the sixteen-pound sledgehammer he used to drive spikes into hard, dry ground. However, when he was soaking wet, he still weighed less than the unwieldy eighty-pound steel rails he carried with some difficulty. Skegami Kitichitaro was only twelve years old. He wasn't an isolated case. The federal census of 1900 lists several Japanese boys living in Uintah County who were as young as thirteen or fourteen.

Working for the railroad was also hard work and dangerous. While the railroads didn't keep records of workers' deaths during the construction of the original Transcontinental Railroad, researchers at Stanford University believe that as many as one thousand unskilled workers died during the construction of the Central Pacific. In addition, a report by the Census Office in 1908 and 1909 said accidental violence caused 52.5 percent of the deaths of untrained railway employees. A study by two sizeable industrial life insurance companies said deaths from accidents in the case of railway track and yard workers were so numerous it obscured all other causes of death in different industries.[17]

Among the Japanese killed in the Wyoming District were James S. Kawamoto, age thirty-six, a section foreman, and S. Sano, age twenty-nine, a section hand. On the day of their deaths, the two men were walking through a deep cut during the winter against a strong wind when they were struck and killed. In addition, an unnamed Japanese laborer employed on a section near Evanston died a peculiar death when a dog hit him after it ran in front of a train and was struck by the cattle catcher and hurled through the air, hitting the Japanese man in the stomach. The victim died several hours later of his injuries.

Weather, living conditions and poor nutrition also contributed to injuries and deaths on the railroad. Wyoming is cold and windy. The average daily temperature throughout the year is less than 42 degrees. The extreme temperature records in Wyoming are a 171-degree swing from a record 61 degrees below zero at Fort Sanders (near Laramie) in 1875 to a sweltering 116 degrees at Bitter Creek in Sweetwater County on July 12, 1900. It's colder if the wind blows. Wyoming's wind is strong enough to twist and bend trees into natural bonsai shapes with a definite lean toward the east or southeast. Winds generally reach speeds of thirty to forty miles per hour and can gust to fifty, sixty or seventy miles per hour or more. Under the right conditions, weather impacts transportation, agriculture and ranching. During the blizzard of 1878, six feet of snow fell during the storm of the century. The blizzard single-handedly wiped out the cattle industry in Wyoming, collapsed the Union Pacific frame car shops in Cheyenne and halted operations in the Wyoming Division of Union Pacific for ten days.

Regardless of the weather, hardships and spartan living conditions, Japanese immigrant section workers earning immigrant wages faithfully kept Union Pacific moving. Teinosuke Endow, a track worker along the Wyoming-Nebraska line, described the solitary and austere life of section workers for the Union Pacific. Endow and his section crew mates lived in an old freight car standing on a sidetrack on the open prairies. His home was more of a sardine can he shared with nine other men. The men slept on the floor on wheat straw and wrapped themselves up in blankets as tight as sushi rolls to trap their body heat. In the morning, as part of their daily routine, the Japanese track workers swept out their metal hovel to eliminate the armies of bedbugs that had assaulted them during the night.

Once a week, a passing train brought them fresh drinking water and food supplies. One passing train dropped wheat flour and bacon, which the men ate daily until the next train dropped off more supplies. Many of the men, if not all, suffered from night blindness because of their unbalanced diet. To supplement their diet, the section workers gathered wild green weeds growing near the railroad tracks and cooked them in a dumpling soup they called *dangoshyuru*. They also bought chickens from a nearby farm and made chicken soup.[18] Japanese section workers also hunted game and fished illegally to add variety to their diet and supplement their nutritional needs.

CHAPTER 4

CHARACTERISTICS OF THE JAPANESE WORKER

Newspapers often described the "Jap" as a failure who was light in physique and staying qualities and lacking in moral steadiness as he was in physical force. But the Japanese were often the immigrant laborer of choice for experienced roadmasters and supervisors because of their strong work ethic, loyalty and potential.

F.W. Green, a roadmaster on the Canadian Pacific Railroad, said:

> *They* [the Japanese] *are quick to learn the work and are intelligent,* [and] *can be used in any kind of track work from putting in switches down to cleaning up or fencing the right of way. They* [the Japanese] *will do any work as cheaply as it can be done by other nationalities. Although it is an unwritten law in this locality not to promote an Asian to foreman, he added, I believe there are a few Japs on the coast who would make good foremen over gangs of their nationality.*[19]

J.A. Ottman, an assistant superintendent for Union Pacific in Cheyenne, also sang the praises of the Japanese. Ottman said the Japanese could efficiently serve as track foremen because they were "far superior to any other foreign nationality and producing more satisfactory results." Ottman explained that in his experience with various classes of foreign labor in the mountainous district of Wyoming, the Japanese produced more satisfactory results because of their ability to manage all types and nationalities because they exhibited a desire to master details and were apt and conscientious scholars who had a facility to impart knowledge to their fellow laborers.

Japanese supervisors also seldom, if ever, repeated an error once brought to their attention, said Ott. Forepersons of other nationalities need this quality, he added.[20] The Union Pacific promoted Japanese to track foremen in 1902 out of necessity because of "a serious condition resulting from the diminishing supply of track labor, and particularly of foremen." Eventually, 96 of the 126 section supervisors in the Wyoming Division of the Union Pacific were Japanese.

Chikahisa Ota was one of those Japanese foremen. Chikahisa Ota was born in Okayama, Japan, in 1887. He immigrated to the United States in 1907 and worked for Union Pacific in Cheyenne before his promotion to section foreman on the Wamsutter line in Sweetwater County. He supervised a crew of mixed nationalities with some success, but there was also interracial tension between the Japanese section laborers and tracklayers of different nationalities. Ota worked as a section foreman until his discharge in 1942 after the Japanese bombed Pearl Harbor airfield in Hawai'i.

One of the reasons Japanese immigrants succeeded on the Union Pacific was because of their ability to assimilate into Western culture by learning English. For example, the Japanese studied how to read and write in English after work. It was an unwritten rule among Japanese track workers to learn at least three words a day to gain a successful command of the English language and idioms. The Japanese also translated Union Pacific work development courses from English to Japanese so all workers fully understood their assignments. As a result, almost 60 percent of the Japanese living in Cheyenne during the 1910 census had some command of English as a second language.

The *Laramie Boomerang* featured a Japanese section worker whom it described as "very intelligent and well educated." Y. Shimaya, age twenty, was a section laborer near Laramie. The *Boomerang* said Shimaya was well acquainted with written English, having learned it at college in Japan, but he was not as acquainted with the spoken language. Shimaya, when asked a question in English, wrote the question down in "good hand using English characters and spelling correctly" so he could understand the question. Shimaya's goal was to enroll at the University of Wyoming and return to Japan to teach English.[21]

As for the Japanese's ability to speak and write in English, that can be traced back to John Mung. Mung, also known as Nakahama Manjiro, was the first Japanese person to visit the United States. He was born on January 27, 1827, in Nakanohama, a fishing village in the Tosa Province (now Kochi Prefecture). A shipwreck left Mung and four fishing friends stranded on an uninhabited island in 1841. They were rescued by the whaling vessel *John Howland* and taken to Hawai'i, where Mung's three friends remained. Mung continued to Fairhaven, Massachusetts, where he lived with Captain William Whitfield and his family. He attended local schools and became proficient in English.

Mung succeeded in his studies and business endeavors, and he eventually captained a whaling ship. But despite his successes, Mung wanted to return to Japan. He did so in 1851 with two friends he had left in Hawai'i. Because leaving Japan was a crime punishable by death, the men were interrogated, released and awarded pensions after the Shogunate learned the truth. Mung became an interpreter and translator for the Shogunate and was instrumental in negotiating the Convention of Kanagawa peace treaty that opened the Western world to Japanese immigration. Mung also taught English, translated English books into Japanese and authored an English phrasebook called *Shortcuts to English Conversation*.

PART II

THE JAPANIZATION OF WYOMING

Union Pacific introduced 393 Japanese immigrants to Wyoming in the early 1900s. Since their arrival, the Japanese immigrant laborers were the unsung heroes for the Union Pacific Railway and the lifeblood of communities along the main line between Cheyenne and Ogden. Japanese labor provided muscle while Union Pacific laid tracks, built steel bridges and stone culverts, lengthened all passing tracks and constructed and maintained new cut-offs that shortened the linear distance between the eastern and western termini of the division. In addition, steam-operated machines reduced the grades at Sherman Hill, Lookout Hill, Simpson Hill and Piedmont Hill and bore tunnels through granite rock faces to eliminate the need for a helper engine to crest grades.[22]

The first installment of Japanese labor in the twentieth century was in Evanston, located in Uintah County. Initially, 160 Japanese people arrived at the headquarters in Evanston, but only 70 lived in Evanston and the surrounding communities of Beckwith, Cokeville, Fossil and Opal. Evanston's Japan Town was on the north side of the railroad tracks on First Street and in an old flour mill fitted up as a "Jap" hotel. One of those residents was a boy known only by the surname of Arda. He was thirteen years old and worked as a railroad laborer for Union Pacific.[23] There were also other boys close to his age assigned as section workers. However, the generally friendly citizens of Evanston didn't welcome the Japanese section hands with open arms; they threatened to blow them to kingdom come.

Japanese laborers refused to report to work after the *Laramie Boomerang* said, "A can of powder was discovered under their [bunk] car, and the little brown men concluded that a conspiracy to blow them up had been formed." The people of Evanston laughed "at the fears of the Japs" and discounted this act of terrorism as just a practical joke. However, Union Pacific took the threat seriously because any work stoppage would affect local, national and global economies. Union Pacific resolved the problem with the help of H. Kishini, an interpreter from Ogden, Utah.[24]

Japanese labor was important to Union Pacific and Evanston. This stretch of track was Union Pacific's version of the new silk road. Union Pacific owned the entire Oriental trade route from Omaha to Yokohama, Japan, and from Ogden, Utah, to Yokohama. Evanston was an important refueling station for cross-country locomotives because of the abundance of timber, water and coal. Union Pacific invested in Evanston by constructing a sixty-five-thousand-square-foot, twenty-eight-stall brick roundhouse, a seventeen-thousand-square-foot brick machine shop, several ancillary buildings and a brick powerhouse with generators. Union Pacific also partnered with the Pacific Fruit Company and built an icehouse in Evanston that employed forty Japanese people.[25]

Eleven miles southeast of Evanston is Altamont. Japanese section workers in this area lived in nearby Hilliard, a prominent lumbering center that manufactured thousands of bushels of charcoal annually. Union Pacific utilized a mixed-nationality workforce in this area composed of one hundred Japanese laborers and a predominantly Greek labor force who worked under Japanese section foreman Sahuichi Yamatisubo. The men overhauled the roadbed between Granger and Piedmont Hill. Union Pacific also built a forty-mile line to detour traffic away from the Aspen Tunnel route in the event of a blockage. The detour bypassed Granger and McCammon Junction in Idaho and connected directly to the Cumberland coal mine line.[26]

Union Pacific also built a cutoff from Leroy to Bear River, reducing the distance by 9.5 miles and the maximum grade per mile, thus eliminating the need for helper engines in both directions at Aspen Tunnel. However, the Aspen Tunnel itself

Men standing on Pacific Express ice cars. Japanese icehouse employees harvested ice from nearby Bear Creek. It cooled fish and California produce destined for markets in the East. *Wyoming State Archives.*

was a shapeshifting nightmare. It sat on a geological stratum of shale of carboniferous formation and sandstone at the infamous Tapioca Hill, known for its shifting geology. Shortly into the tunnel's construction, it filled with water to a depth of seventy feet. Engineers reinforced the tunnel with heavy timbers, but the twelve-by-twelve timbers were twisted, crushed and broken. The tunnel was later reinforced with a steel framework of twelve-inch I-beams overlaid with concrete.[27] There was little local gossip to report from this stretch of railway other than the time T. Miokoto, a Japanese section hand, was run over by the cars at the Aspen Tunnel and had his right leg amputated at a hospital in Ogden in November 1906.[28] There was also a misunderstanding with an Italian steel gang in October 1909 that resulted in the Italian steel gang beating up several Japanese section workers at the tunnel. The Italian ringleader received a $60 fine (equivalent to $2,136.93 in 2023).

The company also employed the Japanese at Fossil. The town of Fossil was fifteen miles west of Kemmerer. Livestock ranchers in this locality depended on Union Pacific to freight cattle and sheep to market. Fossil had a steam-powered sheep shearing plant where an estimated fifty thousand sheep passed through in 1915. There was also a service station and depot, an engine house,

Fossil was once a Union Pacific town, but it's now a ghost town where a Japanese person murdered his fellow countryman. *Wyoming State Archives.*

coal chutes, a pumphouse, a section house and a maintenance house. Additionally, a helper engine assisted eastbound trains over the 10,623-foot Hodges Pass Tunnel. Union Pacific later moved the depot, section house, pumphouse and water tank to a new location a mile west because a steep downgrade east of town caused trains to overshoot the depot. Fossil eventually became a ghost town after Union Pacific relocated its engine house and coal chutes to Kemmerer.[29]

Fossil was also where a Japanese section man brutally murdered a fellow Japanese worker because he "wanted to kill someone." On August 20, 1893, Jiuper Shirai drank heavily. The *Evanston Register* said Shirai was a "bad man, especially when under the influence of alcohol." On the night of the murder, Shirai argued with the victim. He then took a "big" knife and nearly cut his unnamed victim in two. The victim died two days later. Tom Burke, the section foreman, apprehended Shirai, bound him with a rope and placed him in an upstairs room of the section house. However, Shirai managed to cut his bonds and escape. An issued BOLO described Shirai as a short man of Japanese color with a pockmarked face.[30]

Opal is a railroad stop in the Hams Fork River Valley where Japanese section workers lived and worked. Their maintenance of this stretch of railway helped area ranchers ship more than ten thousand head of cattle and sheep and 250,000 pounds of wool to Midwest and eastern markets. Cokeville and Beckwith were also dependent on the Oregon Short Line to move sheep and wool products to market. Cokeville is in the western part of Lincoln County, forty-two miles northwest of Kemmerer. John Bourne located the townsite in 1874. A post office was added in 1881, but the settlement remained a trading post for trappers and Indians until the Oregon Short Line Railroad laid down tracks in the early 1890s, around the time the first Japanese section workers came to Wyoming. The Oregon Short Line built a station at Cokeville, and near the depot a large wool warehouse was constructed. Several million pounds of wool shipped from Cokeville annually.

CHAPTER 5

WYOMING COAL MINES

I n the early days of coal mining in Uintah County, Union Pacific leased coal mining land to the Wyoming Coal and Mining Company. Wyoming Coal then sold coal to UP at a high profit. Union Pacific gained a foothold in the Wyoming coal market after the government terminated the agreement between Wyoming Coal and Union Pacific in 1874.

The coal mining industry was dangerous and was an occupation that did not compensate workers or their families for injury or death. But worker compensation gained momentum after a series of explosions at the Almy mines near Evanston claimed numerous lives. This prompted the Wyoming territorial legislature to pass new mine safety laws. The laws included the inspection of coal mines every three months by the newly created mine inspector office and a ban on women and boys under fourteen years of age from working in mines. Albany County legislator Stephen Downey also recommended compensation for the families of the Almy disaster, but lawmakers voted against it, believing it would set a bad precedent.

In 1915, Wyoming passed a worker's compensation law. However, lawyers in Lincoln County challenged the law after the Japanese widow of R. Morioyono legally received compensation for his death. Morioyono was a rope rider at the mines in Oakley. His job required him to couple steel cables to coal cars and then ride the loaded coal cars out of the mine to the tipple, where they were uncoupled, dumped and processed. On the morning of his death, Morioyono stopped outside the mouth of the mine to converse with two mechanics. When Morioyono restarted the engine, several coal cars

A makeshift morgue. Japanese mining families were compensated in Wyoming's second-worst coal mining accident in 1923. *Frank J. Meyers Papers (5195), American Heritage Center, University of Wyoming.*

broke loose and plunged him down a three-thousand-foot steep incline.[31] Wyoming's Worker's Compensation Law awarded his widow $250. However, a group of lawyers in Lincoln County protested the settlement because they claimed "certain phases of the workmen's compensation law" did not apply to Asians. The lawyers also alleged Japan's government would appropriate the compensation money to fund their military.[32]

There was no challenge, however, to Wyoming's compensation law seven years later when Wyoming awarded survivor benefits compensation to families of Japanese miners killed in the second-worst coal mining accident in Wyoming state history. On August 14, 1923, ninety-nine miners perished in an explosion at the Frontier No. 1 Mine in Kemmerer. Seventeen Japanese miners were among the dead. The State of Wyoming compensated eligible dependents, including wives, children and parents, with payouts that ranged from $80 to more than $3,800. Only eight Japanese miners did not name a next of kin. The compensation paid by the State of Wyoming to surviving Japanese relatives amounted to $9,929.66. Additionally, the Kemmerer Coal Company paid for all mortuary and funeral services.

CHAPTER 6

JAPANESE ASSIMILATION
IN UINTAH COUNTY

The Japanese may have been foreigners in America, but they had an imperial edict from the emperor to obey American laws and be good citizens in their adopted country.[33] Although the Japanese in the coal mining communities of Oakley, Kemmerer and Diamondville lived separately from the townsfolk, people in these close-knit coal communities still thought well enough of the Japanese to include them in community celebrations of national holidays. For example, in 1908, during the Japanese national holiday of the emperor's birthday, bands from Diamondville provided the music, and the citizens of all the coal mining communities in the area turned out for a day of festivities that included clog dancing and sword drills. And the Japanese sponsored the evening fireworks display. Afterward, everyone enjoyed a "fine supper."[34]

Oakley was proud of its diversity. The community's Japanese population numbered sixty-five in 1910. The close-knit communities in Uintah County took time to celebrate Japanese holidays and the successes of its Japanese residents. One of Oakley's more prominent Japanese citizens was H.T. Kubota, a local Japanese agent and "one of the most talented of the foreigners of the West." Kubota settled in the Utah Cache Valley in 1906 to establish a Japanese colony and take up agriculture. However, after two successive years of crop failures, he gave up the pursuit and moved to New York, where he found employment as an assistant bookkeeper with Neilson & Company, a wholesale dealer in white goods. Eight months later, Adkins Clarke Publishing Company offered him a management position to translate all correspondence circulars and books into Japanese. At night, Kubota took bookkeeping and business courses through the International Correspondence School. He earned his diploma in ten months and set all the school records in the bookkeeping and business forms courses. His crowning academic achievement was winning first place at the St. Louis Exposition for his penmanship. Kubota returned to Oakley and started the Wyoming Correspondence School of Penmanship in 1908. His clientele included nine hundred students in Japan and two hundred students in the United States.[35]

The Japanese showed loyalty and appreciation for their adopted community by sponsoring local Fourth of July firework displays and contributing generously to war bond and Red Cross drives. In 1918, the local Japanese residents raised $5,300 for Oakley's third Liberty Loan drive. This is the equivalent of more than $104,000[36] in 2022 dollars.

Many Japanese businesses also thrived in the mining communities of Uintah County. The Japanese American Yearbook in 1910 listed twenty-one Japanese small enterprises. The county had one Japanese-style restaurant and five other Japanese-owned eating establishments that served American meals. The Japanese also operated one barbershop, two photograph studios, five Japanese stores, a pool hall and two laundries. B. Itaya and N. Hayakawa owned one of the more prominent laundries in the county. Itaya and Hayakawa were originally farmers in Japan who moved to Rock Springs and started a laundry business. They moved to Kemmerer in 1909 and opened the Kemmerer Steam Laundry, which became one of the leading steam laundries in western Wyoming. Kemmerer Steam Laundry was a full-service establishment that washed and ironed, cleaned and pressed suits; performed dry and wet work; and delivered laundry by automobile. The business later expanded to accept parcel post packages. Within a decade, the partners had incorporated the business as Kemmerer Union Laundry Company with a capital stock of $25,000, divided into 250 shares valued at $100 each. Five Japanese men—B. Itaya, N. Hayakawa, G. Kaneko, T. Ide and T. Sakihama—served as the directors.[37]

PART III

JAPANESE IN SWEETWATER COUNTY

To the east of Uintah County is Sweetwater County. Union Pacific first introduced Asian labor in its Rock Springs coal mines before the turn of the twentieth century.

Charles Francis Adams, president of Union Pacific Coal Company, described Sweetwater as the salvation of the Union Pacific. He said there was such an abundance of coal that "winter snows turned black." Although UP was not originally in the mining business when the Transcontinental Railroad laid tracks across Wyoming, it acquired area mines from Wyoming Coal and Mining Company. Consequently, Union Pacific gained a monopoly in the coal markets by charging competitors higher freight prices on company-owned rail lines.

Additionally, Union Pacific Coal Company maximized its profits by cutting miners' pay by one-fifth while maintaining the price it charged for selling coal. When miners protested the wage cut and went on strike, Union Pacific Coal replaced them with Chinese laborers who worked for less money.[38]

By 1885, Chinese miners outnumbered white miners in Rock Spring because Pacific Coal "told" its managers to hire only Chinese miners. As resentment for the Chinese grew, posters appeared in railroad towns warning the Chinese to leave Wyoming Territory. Anti-Chinese tension reached critical mass on September 2, 1885. On that morning, white miners killed a Chinese miner in Mine Six with blows of a pick to the skull. The miners also severely beat another Chinese person. Soon the violence spilled into the streets, and women and children joined an angry mob of upward of 150 men as they marched across

Bitter Creek toward China Town, located on the other side of the bend in the railroad tracks. Some men blocked the bridges to prevent the Chinese from fleeing while the rest of the angry mob attacked with guns, knives, hatchets and clubs. A total of 28 Chinese people died in the massacre, and China Town was looted and burned. Only 16 miners were arrested and released because authorities couldn't find witnesses who would swear a crime was even committed.

Chinese leaders in Rock Springs and Evanston urged Union Pacific to pay and discharge the Chinese miners to avert further violence, but the company refused. The company store also refused to sell food or supplies to any Chinese people who did not return to work. Instead, Union Pacific ordered the Chinese to bury their dead and return to the mines. After the riot, Rock Spring's coal fields became more cosmopolitan. By 1910, Rock Springs claimed it was home to fifty-six nationalities. The diversity of nationalities in Rock Springs was an attempt by Union Pacific to prevent races who spoke different languages from unionizing. The majority of the workforce in Rock Springs resembled the immigrants who had settled the land. They were white skinned and hailed from such places as England, Scotland, Wales, Ireland, Finland, Italy, Greece, Slovenia, Serbia, Croatia, Austria, Czechoslovakia, Romania, Hungary and Yugoslavia. Statistically, labor unions couldn't claim Asians took "white man" jobs because the Chinese and Japanese accounted for only 1.3 percent of Rock Spring's population.

Although Rock Springs was diverse, it was segregated by skin tone. While Americans and other white immigrants lived in the city, the Japanese lived on a sagebrush prairie on the outskirts of town. This community was designated on maps as Mine No. 8 Camp or "Jap Camp." The population of Jap Camp was 273. Single males were the predominate group in Jap Camp, but 4 women and 6 children also resided there. In addition, Rock Springs had a second Japanese town with a population of 110 in the vicinity of K Street, Pilot Butte Avenue and Main Street.

Former Jap Camp resident Hyoza Kumagai provided the bulk of understanding of what life was like in Rock Spring's Jap Camp. Kumagai was one of three brothers who called Rock Springs home. He was born in Fukuoka, Japan, in 1892. He immigrated to the United States in 1907, with fifty dollars in his pocket, to work in the coal mines. Kumagai was just fifteen. Miners in those days got up at 2:00 a.m., dressed, ate breakfast and then started for the mines at 2:40 a.m. It took them two hours to cover the four-mile stretch over an uneven and rocky road strewn with sagebrush. When the men finished their ten-hour shifts, they often rode home in an empty coal car.[39]

An average of 252 men worked at Mine No. 8. The Japanese harvested more than 323,200 tons of coal annually with the help of first-class machinery and modern safety devices; however, horses and mules pulled the coal cars out of the coal mines on narrow-gauge steel rails maintained by men such as Nikichi Hamada. The coal was then dumped and transported by an electric locomotive to railway cars for shipment to market.

Nikichi Hamada left his family behind in Japan in 1907 to seek opportunities in the coal mines of Rock Springs. As a common laborer, he pushed cars, shoveled rock and loaded coal cars. He also helped timber the mines and lay track. The job required physical strength, endurance and a willingness

Railroad tracks leading to Mine No. 8. Many Japanese coal miners in Rock Springs worked in Mine No. 8; Union Pacific Wyoming closed the mine on August 28, 1962. *Wyoming State Archives.*

A Japanese family: Haruye (Hirayama) Hamada (*seated, left*), John Hatsuki Hamada, Bill Hamada (*standing in front*), Nikichi Hamada, Jeanne Hamada, Momoye Hamada and Asa Hamada. *Courtesy of Don Aoki.*

to work in an underground environment where there is no natural light and ventilation is a mechanical process. To keep pace with the tonnage of coal mined, Nikichi and other track workers continually maintained or replaced sixty-pound rails. They ensured rails were spaced eighteen inches from center to center on the hardwood ties, and the crew aligned tracks on the straightaways and curves by ballasting ties and tamping spikes and plates to prevent the rails from springing up or spreading as heavy coal cars passed over them. One day, a cart loaded with coal rolled down a hill. After Nikichi watched several of his fellow laborers make futile attempts to pull the cart up the incline, he attempted to rescue the runaway cart by himself. Nikichi didn't have the typical slight build of his countrymen; he was tall and muscularly built. He looked like a Japanese version of Superman.

Nikichi surveyed the situation and then strapped himself into a harness and attached it to the runaway cart. He spread his feet about shoulder-width apart and placed one powerful leg in front of his body, much the way a sprinter takes a stance before a race. Nikichi then bent his hips slightly, keeping his head, chest

John and Asa Hamada (wearing the feather hat). John worked as a paymaster for the coal mine, and Asa Hamada told ghost stories. Meiji died and is buried in Rock Springs. *Courtesy of Don Aoki.*

and spine in a neutral position. Then, he pumped his arms and pushed off his toes in slow motion to gain momentum. As he lurched forward, the slack tightened on the cart behind him, and the lactic acid built up in his calves. Soon there was a squeaking sound of metal on metal as the heavily laden cart moved. Then, finally, Nikichi did the impossible—he pulled the cart to the level ground by himself.

In other demonstrations of strength, Nikichi carried a rail segment the farthest, and he was the only man in the Rock

Nikichi Hamada's pay stub. Nikichi Hamada (#1031) earned 43½ cents an hour working for Union Pacific Coal Company, the equivalent of $13.92 in 2023. *Courtesy of Don Aoki.*

Springs coal camps who could pull a coal car by his teeth. Union Pacific later promoted Nikichi and gave him a 2½-cent wage increase to 43 cents an hour. Soon Nikichi saved enough money to bring his wife, Asa, and their three children to Rock Springs in 1914.

Hatsuki Hamada, who adopted the name John, was one of Nikichi's children. John graduated from high school in Japan, but he also attended high school in Rock Springs to better his English and develop necessary skills to assimilate into American society. He later worked for Union Pacific Coal Company as a paymaster. His job as paymaster required him to walk into town, pick up the payroll and deliver large sums of cash to the mines. This was a dangerous job because there were still men who followed in the footsteps of Butch Cassidy. Butch earned his moniker working as an apprentice butcher in Rock Springs, but he and his outlaws were better known for robbing banks and trains. At nearby Wilcox, his men allegedly blew up a train when they tried to open a safe with dynamite. Outlaws knew that waylaying a paymaster during their thirty-minute walk from the mining camps was a quick payday.

On one snowy day, John noticed a man with a rifle following him after he had picked up the payroll. John was not tall or muscle-bound like his father. Instead, he relied on his wits and made it appear that he vanished into thin air. He did this by retracing his footsteps in the snow and then hiding behind a boulder. When the highwayman reached the end of the tracks, he scratched his head and looked around in confusion. In another close call, John arrived in town shortly after an outlaw robbed a bank on Front Street. A sheriff leaving a nearby saloon gunned down the desperado.[40]

Shortly after the robberies, the family left for Sacramento, California, following the deaths of two young family members. The Hamadas' youngest son, Hideo, died from hypothermia during one of Rock Springs' coldest winters. He was just eleven days old. His brother Meiji, who came to Rock Springs in 1914, died the following year from diphtheria.

CHAPTER 7

ENTERTAINMENT IN JAP CAMP

G ambling and drinking were the main pastimes in Japanese colonies along the Union Pacific, even after the Wyoming legislature banned legalized gambling on January 1, 1902, and passed a prohibition on alcohol. When Jap Camp boss Chikanori Gondow prohibited gambling in the camp in 1909, four men showed their displeasure by going to the colony headquarters to beat some sense into Gondow. They were later arrested and charged with malicious destruction because when they couldn't find Gondow, the *Cheyenne Daily Leader* said the men instead "Jiu-Jitsued" the office, destroying furniture, books and records.[41]

Before Prohibition, the camp men used to buy their liquor from an old Italian man named Miko. He sold liquor from a cart pulled by an emaciated horse. Miko continued to make his rounds at Jap Camp, always leaving with a pocket full of money. When the temperance movement ended the open sale of alcohol, the men made their own hooch, using a concoction of fermented rice and yeast and fermenting it in a fifty-gallon barrel that once held soy sauce.[42]

Jap Camp also had family-oriented entertainment. On warm summer nights, a crowd between fifty and sixty gathered on a gentle slope near the camp for an evening of entertainment. People such as Shichigoro Hirayama and Asa Hamada recited newspaper articles and performed for the crowd. Hirayama and Hamada are the great-grandparents of Don Aoki, a fourth-generation Californian, whose short film *Pioneers of Wyoming* pays tribute to his fifteen Japanese ancestors who called Rock Springs home during the first two decades of the twentieth century.

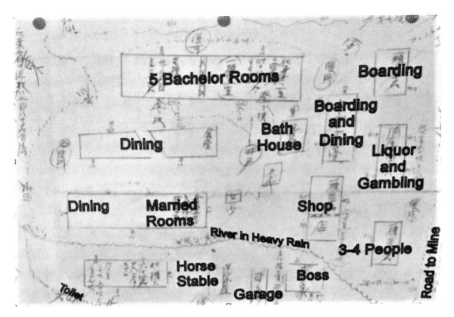

A map of Jap Camp, which was on a sagebrush-covered prairie near Mine No. 8. Miners often crowded into long wooden barracks to save money. *Rock Springs Historical Museum.*

Shichigoro was one of the few English-speaking residents of Jap Camp; he often recited news from the local papers and retold amusing old Japanese stories. He came to Rock Springs in 1904 with his wife, Shima, and daughter, Haruye, to escape the brutal conditions of working on a sugar plantation in Maui, Hawai'i. Instead, Hirayama worked in the coal mines of Union Pacific Coal Company. While the work was dangerous, it was preferable to working for sugar plantation overseers who imposed harsh fines and whippings for talking, smoking or pausing to stretch in the fields. And there was Asa Hamada; she was a natural-born entertainer. Asa was popular among children because she was adept at telling Japanese ghost stories. And she often performed for the local grocers in pantomime to communicate her grocery needs because she didn't speak English. Whenever she wanted eggs, she squatted down, flapped her arms wildly and mimicked a hen depositing an egg.[43]

Jap Camp also celebrated traditional Japanese holidays. Occasionally, the citizens of Rock Springs joined in the celebration. For example, Rock Springs citizens helped celebrate a Japanese naval victory at Port Arthur, Philippines, during the Japanese-Russo War. The Rock Springs Saxophone Band led a nighttime procession of floats that streamed past four hundred Japanese people holding paper lanterns. One of the floats resembled a

Japanese navy battleship. Its mounted guns shot fireworks, creating shapes of humans, animals, birds and dragons.[44]

When all the Japanese colonies along the Union Pacific celebrated Emperor Mutsuhito's birthday, the Japanese labor agency Wakimoto and Nishimura helped defray the cost of the celebration by sending cash presents to each Japanese section house along the line to pay for a generally held feast.[45]

Unfortunately, the Swedes employed at the Angell and George quarry east of Laramie were fired from their jobs when they joined the Japanese in a celebration. The Swedes at the quarry believed "the Japs had gone out for more pay or something." So, they laid down their tools and joined in a "sympathy strike." The Japanese resumed work the following morning, but the quarry paid off the Swedes and fired them.[46]

CHAPTER 8

JAP CAMP FOOD

Hyoza Kumagai said half of the men living in the Jap Camp took their meals at a boardinghouse managed by the boss, or they ate at four other places in the camp. Rice and rabbit were some of the staples. The rice available in camp was a type called *tomai*. It was poor-quality rice, but it was reasonably priced and smelly. Meals in Jap Camp were simple. There were generally pieces of meat and gobo, a special kind of Japanese herb used for cooking. They also ate napa cabbage, spinach and bean-curd (miso) soup. On Sundays, the Japanese served American-style meals. These meals generally consisted of a small-size steak, two pieces of potato and ketchup. The rabbit was also an abundant and easily hunted protein source. Kumagai said he didn't hunt rabbits with a rifle; instead, he designed a sixteen-foot-long wire with a barbed end that he and his friends used to fish rabbits out of their holes.

There was also a married couple in camp who hosted more gourmet meals for the fifteen to twenty people who paid two dollars each to employ the wife as a cook. This impromptu dinner club bought Chinese cabbage, onions, Japanese daikon radishes and soybeans from a Chinese peddler named Chan, who came by the camp twice a week.[47] The wife paired the vegetables with tuna, sea bass, sardines and other fresh fish purchased from Tsuruji (Kakuji) Okano, who owned a fish market on Pilot Butte Street.[48]

Okano, the local fishmonger, was born in Hiroshima, Japan, on April 1, 1890. At sixteen, he immigrated to Seattle, Washington, and then removed to the coal mine camp at Rock Springs. Okano sold fish caught on the West

A train approaching Wilkins Switch. The *Wyoming Star* reported that Japanese and Greek laborers clashed near Wilkins in September 1905. Law enforcement arrested eleven "Japs." *Wyoming State Archives.*

Coast the day before. The daily catch was packed in ice and shipped by railway express to Okano's fish market within eighteen hours of being caught. After he received fish shipments every Wednesday, Okano prepped the catch and sold it on Fridays to a cosmopolitan clientele that included Japanese, Chinese, Greek and Slovenian immigrants and anyone of the Catholic faith, who traditionally ate fish on meatless Fridays. The Greeks were especially helpful to Kakuji because he didn't speak English. On Fridays, when his Greek customers came in, they pointed to the fish and told Okano the name of it. Kakuji then wrote down the name and displayed it next to the fish.

On Saturdays, his wife, Misao Funayama Okano, managed the market while Okano and his son George peddled fresh fish and other goods to Japanese section hands at Bryan Station, just west of Green River. They often left home early in the morning and didn't return until late at night. In addition, Okano visited crews east of Rock Springs at Wamsutter, Dienes, Winton and Superior on Mondays and Tuesdays.[49]

CHAPTER 9

THE JAPANESE JOIN THE UNION

I n 1907, the United States and Japan reached an informal agreement restricting the inflow of Japanese immigrants. This was a diplomatic move by President Theodore Roosevelt to address growing anti-Japanese sentiment in California. While America restricted Japanese labor, unions in Rock Springs wanted the Chinese and Japanese to join the local associations. There were forty-three nationalities living in Rock Springs at the time who were members of the United Mine Workers of America union; however, the *Cheyenne Daily Leader* pointed out that there were no "Chinks or Japs."[50]

Every coal mine at Rock Springs was closed in 1907 because of a strike. Over two thousand men called for their time and were told to vacate company-owned housing, while the Union Pacific tried to get non-union men from the East to reopen the mines.[51]

When the Unions "noticed" the Japanese were sympathetic to the striking miners, they passed a resolution and held membership drives in the various camps. Japanese leaders initially resisted any connection with the union campaign. However, General Nishiyama, one of the foremost Intermountain leaders, was influential in getting Japanese miners to join the union and in sending delegates to the Denver union convention.[52] The convention was the first district meeting since the Chinese Massacre in 1885. As a result, the Chinese and Japanese received a special dispensation and entry into the local mining associations.

Jap Camp boss Chikanori Gondow and R. Suzoki were the two Japanese people who represented about six hundred union Japanese miners at the

Denver Conference. As a result of the negotiations, Union members agreed to an eight-hour workday, improved working conditions and a pay raise. For Japanese miners in Wyoming, this meant a dollar raise to $3.10 (some sources say $3.25). Finally, the Japanese coal miners in Wyoming achieved equality with their white brethren, and they were now among the highest paid in the western states.

RELIANCE AND SUPERIOR

Reliance was a coal camp in Sweetwater County, five miles north of Rock Springs. It was almost as culturally as diverse as Rock Springs, with nearly twenty different nationalities. The town of Superior is north of Reliance.

In 1903, Union Pacific constructed a railroad from Thayer Junction on the main line to Superior, and the company built a depot. Five coal mines at Superior named A, B, C, D and E operated under the banner of Superior Coal Company. The Japanese lived and worked in A Camp. The mine was

Railroad leading to UPCC mine dump. Superior had twenty nationalities working its mines. The Japanese lived in a segregated town near Mine A. It had stores and schools. *Wyoming State Archives.*

in a small canyon just south of Superior, and it had a school and a company store. Reliance and Superior merged into one town in 1906; in 1916, Union Pacific Coal Company bought out the Superior Coal Company. There was no running water in south Superior in the good old days. The available water was nonpotable from the mine and was murky and inky. Any water for domestic use was hauled by wagon from local springs and sold for twenty-five cents a barrel. Whenever the town girls washed their hair, they had to go to the machine shop to get hot water from the steam pipes.

The Union Pacific eventually hauled water from the small community of Point of Rocks, and Union Pacific moved the water in tank cars. However, the freighting of fresh water made the water quite expensive, so the citizens queued up at a water pump in South Superior and carried their water home in five-gallon buckets until World War I.

CHAPTER 10

SUPERIOR'S JAPANESE
FIRST AID TEAM

B ecause coal mining was a hazardous occupation, Union Pacific
Coal Company formed several first aid response teams to rescue
injured miners. The men were all members of the United Mine
Workers of America, District No. 22. A Japanese first aid and mine-rescue
team at Superior was the first and only fully trained Japanese squad in
the nation.

The first aid teams met after hours to learn first aid and how to rescue
trapped and injured miners. As a result, the program increased the
survivability of injured men and drew the commendations of doctors who
treated the injured. First aid teams operated out of a remodeled coach
specially equipped for rescue. The rescue coach had a modern kitchen with
water tanks; a sink; a steel range; a cupboard; six berths; lockers for blankets,
bedding, rescue apparatus, first-aid material, flashlights, batteries, railway
and marine fire extinguishers and safety lamps; army field stretchers; a lung
motor; a mouth-breathing apparatus; a half-hour self-rescuer breathing
apparatus; and other necessary equipment for use in case of an accident.[53]

Union Pacific also hosted first aid competitions that required contestants to
treat one or multiple patients injured in various mining accident scenarios. In
addition, Union Pacific awarded cash, medals and other prizes for categories
such as full team events, two-man events and one-man events.

In the full team events, club teams had to solve four problems with the
least number of demerits. After scores were tallied, Union Pacific awarded
thirty dollars and individual gold medals for first place, twenty dollars and

Men in front of a railroad car first aid team in 1916. The Japanese team included C.N. Sunada, Y. Ogasawara, T. Furushiro, I. Tashima and M. Sunada. *Permission by Steve Fiscor, Coal Age.*

silver medals for second place and fifteen dollars for third place. Two-man events paid out fifteen dollars for the first-place team, a ten-dollar pair of pants for the second-place team and a five-dollar pair of trousers for third place. The one-man event place winners received a fifteen-dollar suit of clothes for first place, a ten-dollar pair of shoes for second place and eight dollars in merchandise for third. Other field day events included an entire team event for novices, comical first aid stunt teams, a wire rope and power line splicing contest, a timberman's competition, a tracklayer's competition, a catching-the-greasy-pig contest and fat man and old man races. There was also a Japanese and Chinese race where contestants could win five dollars in merchandise for finishing first and three dollars for second place.[54]

PART IV

JAPANESE IN CARBON COUNTY

When Union Pacific brought 160 Japanese laborers for work between Ogden and Carbon County in 1900, the county seat of Rawlins was the only town that did not receive a "shipment of brown men." Eventually, 32 Japanese workers called the town home, but their stay was short-lived. The town was proud that "for many years Rawlins has placed a ban on the yellow race, and both Mongolians and Japanese have found it impossible to live in town owing to the abuse heaped upon them, not as a body of people but as individuals."[55]

Many of the town's residents were rough and broken, and they should have been incarcerated at the local state penitentiary for the hatred and abuse inflicted on the small Asian community. Rawlins was proud of the fact that the Chinese workers had left several years earlier, and now, any Asian who drifted into their prairie paradise of sagebrush and alkali-flecked soil was beaten because of the color of their skin. In February 1902, the *Cheyenne Daily Leader* reported that "three disciples of the Mikado" were assaulted. Frank Osaky was one of the Japanese men beaten. He was jumped by "drunk rowdies" and repeatedly kicked in the head. He required several stitches to close the gash.[56] Less than a month later, all the Japanese in Rawlins packed their bags and left.[57]

In 1903, Union Pacific sent the Japanese back into the tiger's den. The Union Pacific director, Edward Henry Harriman, placed a big order for 100,000 tons of eighty-five-pound steel rail. This was enough rails to double-track 755 miles and leave enough for several hundred miles of extensions or improvements.[58] Rawlins had been essential to Union Pacific since the Transcontinental Railroad days. Union Pacific built a hotel, a fifteen-stall roundhouse and a machine shop. County stock producers, farmers, silver miners and red metallic paint miners and manufacturers all benefited from Union Pacific's presence. Under Harriman's watch, Union Pacific erected a new twenty-stall roundhouse, and Harriman wanted to relocate and lay 42.83 miles of new track between Rawlins and Tipton.

The *Cheyenne Daily Leader* of December 1903 said the railroad couldn't hire enough white men to manage the section, so Union Pacific turned to the Japanese again.[59] By the 1910 census, there were forty-three Japanese people living near the tracks at East Front Street. In 1917, the Japanese community sponsored the local Independence Day fireworks display.[60]

CHAPTER 11

TRAIN WRECK AT DANA

Dana was an unimportant station in Carbon County. There were eighteen Japanese people living in Dana in 1900. The Japanese section crew was responsible for maintaining the line from Allen Junction to Dana. That is, until the section crew "ran for the hills" after a train derailment west of the switch on January 26, 1909. This wasn't the first time a party responsible for causing a train accident fled the scene. In November 1904, Frank Miller, an operator at Granger, fled after twelve people died when the Pacific Express No. 3 and an extra eastbound fruit train collided head-on at Azusu station.

On the day of the Dana accident, the Japanese section gang pulled up spikes on a section of rail located on a sharp curve about two hundred yards west of the switch. The *Saratoga Sun* wrote that the section gang, "it seems," put up a red flag to notify approaching trains of the rail replacement, but heavy winds blew the flag down before an oncoming passenger train came to the missing section of track.[61] An inquiry board, however, laid the blame on the section foreman for failure to put up a warning flag before the Portland Limited approached the curve at full speed. Three passengers died and thirty were injured when the Portland Limited engine and nine cars derailed into a ditch.[62]

While people pointed an accusing finger at the Japanese, they couldn't legally be punished because there were no laws in Wyoming holding them accountable for the accident. The Wyoming legislature, which was in session when the accident occurred, also failed to enact any law to punish Union Pacific employees for gross negligence.

CHAPTER 12

JAPANESE IN HANNA

Hanna was a coal mining town founded in 1889. The Wakimoto-Nishimura Company of Cheyenne supplied the Union Pacific Coal Company with an estimated five hundred Japanese laborers. The agency charged $1.50 per month in commission fees and also received five-sixths of a percent on the product mined. Union Pacific owned everything in Hanna. The company charged miners $18 monthly for a six-room cottage, which was equivalent to one week's wage.[63] The town did not have an adequate sewer system, so on many occasions, foul water seeped

Hanna Mine No. 2. Japanese coal miners in Hanna lived near Mine No. 2. Japan Town had its own store and school. *Wyoming State Archives.*

Rolling Mill. Some Japanese people left coal mining in Hanna to work at the rolling mill in Laramie during a coal mine strike. *Wyoming State Archives.*

into the cellars of all the buildings on the main street. The stench was so vile that residents used carbolic acid and other disinfectants to kill the smell.

In September 1908, freight traffic in the Wyoming Division decreased by 25 percent when Japanese miners joined the southern Wyoming coal miners' strike. During the strike, Japanese laborers found jobs in the beet fields of Colorado and Kansas and at the rolling mill in Laramie. In the aftermath of the strike, only 120 Japanese lived in Hanna when mining operations resumed.[64]

PART V

JAPANESE IN ALBANY COUNTY

"The Japs Are Coming." This warning in the *Laramie Boomerang* newspaper from April 30, 1900, was reminiscent of Paul Revere's midnight ride to warn colonists of an impending British invasion.

In 1900, Union Pacific labor agent Martin O'Malley introduced thirteen Japanese workers to Laramie. The Japanese community in Albany County grew fast in the same year because Union Pacific and other railways in the area used the Japanese as both section workers and strikebreakers. In early May 1900, a "force of 40 Japanese laborers" from Evanston had replaced striking Italians on a section of grade fourteen miles west of Laramie.[65] The strike was the second by the Italian steel gang. The strike became violent when the crew threatened the section foreman with guns and knives. Local law enforcement monitored the transfer of duties. Still, the *Wyoming Tribune* predicted that if the Italians picked a fight with the "little fellows from the 'Flowery Kingdom,'" the Japanese would "do the others up" because "they [the Japanese] are said to be fighters from Wayback, Japan."[66]

When the 1910 census was enumerated, forty-seven Japanese lived in Laramie. They lived in the confines of the railroad yard, and marginalia on the 1910 census form said, "These men live in boxcars." The general tone of this statement indicates the Japanese lived in spartan conditions. However, at the time, Union Pacific was converting boxcars into containerized tiny houses with sixteen bunks arranged along the walls. Other modified boxcars served as dining cars and showers.[67]

The Japanese also lived in a boardinghouse on Third Street, near Union Pacific's rolling mill. Union Pacific built the rolling mill in 1875 for $250,000. It employed two hundred men at the mill to convert twenty thousand tons of old steel rails and equipment into shiny new tracks. The company also had an extensive car shop.

In 1908, a race war between Japanese immigrants and whites broke out in Laramie. This ethnocentric aggression followed on the heels of the Pacific coast riots in San Francisco, California; Bellingham, Washington; and Vancouver, British Columbia. Friday the Thirteenth 1908 was a bad luck day for Japanese residents of Laramie. Juvenile miscreants hurled rocks and broke windows and lights at a "Jap" boardinghouse near the rolling mill during four days of aggression. The *Laramie Boomerang* reported, "There was no clue to the perpetrators of the deed, but it was a foregone conclusion that it was done by whites."

On the second day of the riot, boys between the ages of fourteen and seventeen roped and dragged "a Jap passing up Third street." Several boys then taunted and harassed Japanese workers in a Second Street poolroom the following day.[68]

Boxcar living. Some Japanese section workers lived in boxcars on railroad property. Over time, Union Pacific remodeled boxcars to make them more livable. *Author's collection.*

The reason for the violent outbursts became apparent on Monday. J. Will Highleyman, a foreman for the Wyoming District, fired several Japanese engine wipers and other shop laborers and replaced them with twenty-five Americans who had lost their jobs a few days prior. The *Semi-Weekly Boomerang* noted, "This is the first move of this kind that has been made along the Union Pacific and it was largely due to Mr. Highleyman's desire to see the white man employed that the order allowing the changes to be made was secure."[69]

CHAPTER 13

GRAND AVENUE WATER PROJECT

Shortly after the Laramie riots, ninety Japanese workers for Union Pacific constructed a new water main on Grand Avenue in May 1908. When the Transcontinental Railroad laid tracks across Wyoming, water was a serious question. Some trains along the line were supplied with water by extra trains, and the remaining water was stored in specially constructed frost-proof iron column water tanks. However, this was expensive. Union Pacific's board of directors resolved the water dilemma by tapping into the area's natural water supply from springs and artesian wells. The old water pipe on Grand Avenue leaked badly, and the local marshal had his hands full with the overflow discharge of water down the streets. As a result, city officials condemned the timeworn waterworks because they worried that certain city sections would flood if a hard freeze occurred.[70]

Union Pacific dug a trench from the Laramie River to the city limits using Japanese laborers. After opening up more than two hundred yards of the earth during the first afternoon of work, the crew laid the pipe and then closed up the ditch, leaving construction in downtown Laramie thoroughfares until last to avoid traffic inconveniences. The Japanese were so efficient that the *Laramie Boomerang* said, "If this gait is maintained, the Japanese crew should complete the project in six weeks." The work, however, was subject to controversy. The Laramie Commercial Club petitioned Union Pacific to employ white men for the water main project.[71]

The *Boomerang* reported a month later that the Grand Avenue pipeline was connected from the springs to the downtown district and neared completion. "The laying of the main has been done in remarkably short time. Work was commenced on May 16 with nearly 100 Japs employed." They completed the project in five weeks. After the construction, Laramie residents in nearby neighborhoods petitioned Laramie City Council to connect to the water main.[72]

Another railroad company that operated in Albany County was the Laramie, Hahn's Peak and Pacific Railroad. The LHP&P Railroad was the vision of Boston banker and businessman Isaac Van Horn. Van Horn wanted to build a rail line between Laramie and Coalmont, Colorado. There was also a plan to connect to the Pacific coast. Van Horn filed articles of incorporation for LHP&P in the Albany County Courthouse in Laramie on February 27, 1901. Construction on the railway proved challenging because of steep terrain up to 9,055 feet above sea level and the need for numerous curves. LHP&P initially hired seventy-five Greek track laborers to build the road, but the company discharged them after they threatened violence because some of their numbers had to pay a railroad fare to travel from Laramie to grading camps near Centennial.[73]

The railway replaced striking Greeks with Japanese section workers. When construction was completed in November 1911, the railway connected isolated gold, copper and coal mining and ranching communities to the Union Pacific. But Laramie, Hahn's Peak and Pacific did not turn a profit. The cost of construction and the continued cost of maintaining the line during the winter forced the company into receivership. An example of Hahn's Peak's winter woes includes the time Japanese laborers dug two engines out of the snow on the Hahn's Peak Road in the Harrison cut, two miles south of Albany station. During one particularly heavy snow in March, an inbound train was buried at the Harrison cut. The engine had followed a plow as it bored a tunnel through colossal drifts, but the snow walls on both sides collapsed and buried both engines, two cattle cars and a bunk car beneath sixty-five feet of snow.[74] It took several days for the Japanese rescuers to extricate several men trapped in a bunk car and all the cattle.

The line was later purchased by John W. Dixon of the Guaranty Trust in May 1914. Since then, the line operated under the names Colorado, Wyoming and Eastern Railway Company (1914–24), Northern Colorado and Eastern Railroad Company (1924) and Western Railroad Company. Union Pacific finally took over the operations in 1936.

The Denver, Laramie and Northwestern was another emerging railroad company at the time. DL&NW also envisioned connecting Wyoming to the Pacific coast. DL&NW wanted to run a line parallel to Union Pacific from

A rotary train in snow. Japanese laborers unburied a rotary train and engine with cars from sixty-five feet of snow, saving several men and carloads of cattle. *Wyoming State Archives.*

Union Pacific eliminated Dale Creek Trestle Bridge (pictured here) and filled the canyons with more than 500,000 cubic yards of fill material. *Wyoming State Archives.*

Denver to Laramie, up to the southwest corner of Yellowstone National Park and into Seattle.[75] DL&NW incorporated in Wyoming on March 5, 1906; however, the company dissolved in 1917 because of financial difficulties.

To the east of Laramie, Union Pacific undertook one of the heaviest railroad grading projects from Laramie to Buford. The new grade crossed the old line in a cut at Tie Siding. The project extended the overall rail length by 0.37 miles, but it reduced the maximum rise from 97.68 feet per mile to 43.3 feet per mile. In addition, the project shaved the highest elevation on the Transcontinental Railroad at Sherman Hill from 8,247 feet to 8,000 feet.

The line deviation also eliminated the famous Dale Creek trestle bridge, an engineering marvel constructed during the original building of the Transcontinental Railroad. Dale Creek Bridge towered 135 feet high over the creek and spanned 650 feet from bluff to bluff. Union Pacific filled the tremendously deep canyons with more than 500,000 cubic yards of fill material and installed an immense drainage system of concrete and iron pipe culverts. The two embankments adjacent to the Dale Creek fill required 250,000 cubic yards. At Lone Tree Creek, Union Pacific filled the 130-foot-deep crevasses with more than 350,000 cubic yards of fill. At Sherman Hill, Union Pacific excavated through 1,800 feet of solid granite to build a tunnel and built a 3,000-foot tunnel just east of Tie Siding.

CHAPTER 14

CARBON TIMBER COMPANY

C arbon Timber Company hired twenty-five Japanese laborers in July 1907. The camp was in the Medicine Bow Forest Reserve, south of Encampment, and it straddled the Wyoming and Colorado borders. Elevations at the tie camp ranged from 8,200 feet at Douglas Creek to almost 10,000 feet at the mining claims in the north.

Carbon Timber Company had a headquarters at Hanna, Wyoming. Between 1905 and 1906, the company operated two camps within the reserve, one being the French Creek Tie Camp on Barrett Creek, at the northern end of the reserve. The second camp was Douglas Creek Camp on Devils Gate Creek. At Douglas Creek, there were commissary buildings, a cookhouse, a blacksmith shop, ranger's cabins and stables. The Japanese who worked in the camps were hired in Denver to pile brush in the Douglas Creek tie camp. After the men learned the business, they became choppers themselves. The *Laramie Republican* said, "Several hundred of these laborers will be added to the force as they are needed, white labor being impossible to secure at this time."

Japanese laborers cleaned up the debris from chips, "juggles" and small branches and piled the debris around tree stumps and burned them under the guidance of the forest service. This work was essential to lower the risk of a forest fire spreading, as it did in 1902, when the most disastrous forest fire in the history of the Sierra Madre Range raged twelve miles south of Grand Encampment. The fire destroyed an estimated nine million feet of timber estimated at thousands of dollars.[76] As a result, all timber camp employees,

Ties at Fort Steele. Japanese tie hacks worked in the Medicine Bow Forest Reserves. Ties were water expressed to Fort Steele at the end of the season. *Wyoming State Archives.*

including the Japanese, pulled double duty as wildland firefighters. The company also assigned the Japanese to Fort Steele for the tie drive down the North Platte River.[77]

The Union Pacific purchased 1 million ties annually, 600,000 of which came from the Medicine Bow and Sierra Madre Mountains. Union Pacific paid 39 cents for lodgepole pine standard ties delivered at Fort Steele and loaded on the cars. The company bought culls for 25 cents to construct snow guards. Union Pacific Coal Company purchased between 150,000 and 175,000 pieces of mining timber for $2\frac{3}{4}$ cents per lineal foot.[78]

Carbon Timber employed about three hundred tie makers and loggers annually.[79] Choppers felled the trees, and tie makers cleared branches, scored the logs and hewed them along two sides in parallel faces. Tie makers then sawed the logs into eight-foot lengths for ties to a diameter of nine to ten inches. The remainder of the raw lumber, down to six inches in diameter, became mining timber. Both railroad and mining ties were then peeled and piled near a road for inspection by a timber boss.

Ties destined for railroad use were floated down Douglas Creek to the North Platte River in June and then driven fifty miles down the Platte to a tie-loading plant at Fort Steele. Workers used a crossbar with chains and spikes at the plant to capture the ties and move them to a chute where men with pike poles funneled floating logs past railroad inspectors. Finally, four men loaded and stacked the ties into a railcar if the tie passed inspection.

Inspectors rejected ties with defects or those that were undersized. Logs not properly peeled were pulled to a loading platform, finished and inspected a second time. Ties designated for mining were shipped to Laramie and treated with preservatives and then sent to the several mines of the Union Pacific Coal Company.

Carbon Timber Company continued to supply ties and mining timber to Union Pacific until 1913.

CHAPTER 15

HEIGORO ENDO

Heigoro Endo is the paternal grandfather of Professor Russell Endo, a noted scholar, lecturer and author about Colorado's Japanese history. Heigoro worked on a stretch of the railway north of Laramie from the spring of 1900 to September 1901.

Heigoro was born in Japan's Shizuoka Ken Prefecture, a picturesque region sometimes referred to as Japan's Riviera. Shizuoka Prefecture sits along the Pacific coast in the south of the Chubu region, which is famous for its mandarin oranges, quality Japanese green tea, hot springs and the postcard-perfect Mount Fuji. Heigoro and other family members left Japan from the port of Yokohama aboard the SS *Goodwin* on March 29, 1900. The *Goodwin* docked at Tacoma, Washington, on April 17, 1900. When Heigoro disembarked, he had thirty-five dollars and a student visa.

His first job in his adopted country was with the Union Pacific at Howell, Wyoming. He was fourteen and a half years old at the time. At Howell, Union Pacific built a 3,900-foot-long passing track parallel to the main line between Laramie and Howell. These sidings enabled two long freight trains running in opposite directions to pass a train of superior class without interference. The Union Pacific also built a 15.34-mile-long cutoff in the dark gray Benton shale from Howell to Hutton's. This new cutoff saved 3.11 miles. Howell to Hutton also reduced the number of curves to one and the maximum grade by 42.2 feet per mile. The heaviest earthwork on this cutoff was at the Foot Creek fill, which spanned 2,000 feet at a depth of 40 feet.

Heigoro Endo playing cards as an adult. He was fourteen and a half years old when he worked for Union Pacific as a section man at Howell, Wyoming. *Courtesy of Russ Endo.*

Crofutt's Overland Tourist described Howell as "an unimportant station on the Union Pacific where trains seldom stop." The only excitement to write home about was the day sparks from an engine became a fire that engulfed thirty-nine cars carrying horses on August 16, 1900. Railroad workers had to cut the forward end of the train loose and sidetracked it at the soda works. They pried open the doors, and the horses jumped to safety. Unfortunately, four horses died in the fire, and several others were injured while jumping.[80]

CHAPTER 16

WYOMING'S MISCEGENATION LAW

Miscegenation is the interbreeding of people of different racial types. It's hard to believe that under Wyoming's miscegenation laws, it was a felony for a white woman to marry a Japanese man. Wyoming first recognized the ban on interracial marriage in 1869. The law stated that "any person belonging to the Caucasian or white race, who shall hereafter knowingly intermarry with a person of one-eight, or more negro, Asiatic, or Mongolian blood, shall be deemed guilty of a felony, and upon conviction thereof shall be punished by imprisonment in the penitentiary not less than three, nor more than seven years." Under Wyoming's miscegenation law, a Japanese person found guilty of trying to intermarry with a white person, upon conviction, could be imprisoned for not less than one or more than five years.[81]

Wyoming repealed the law around the time of the Chinese Exclusion Act, but the state unanimously passed a new version of the miscegenation law in February 1913 because of Japanese immigrants. Between 1909 and 1910, the Albany County clerk's office issued four licenses to interracial couples. In 1909, Suyeki Yamada and Carrie Newman, both of Denver, Colorado, traveled to Laramie to apply for a marriage license. When asked why the couple married in another state, Newman Yamada said that "she and the Jap had come to Laramie to avoid interference of friends" who opposed the match.

Yamada and Johnson appeared at the county clerk's office and made a license application. The county clerk did not issue a marriage license because he was unsure whether he had the authority to give a marriage license to an interracial couple. It took a judge to determine whether the couple had a legal right to marry. When the matter was resolved, the Albany County clerk also issued marriage licenses to Bill Sakata and Dora Waller and Harrie Watanabe and Mabel Osborne.[82] All three couples, who married that day, divorced shortly after the weddings.

In 1910, Carrie Newman Yamada petitioned a divorce from Suyeki Yamada. She accused her husband of "taking her diamonds and using the money which she had saved by a life of shame to start a Japanese gambling house" in Denver. She also claimed Yamada had attempted to kill her because she wouldn't agree to withdraw her contest of a suit for divorce and $2,000 in alimony.[83] Yamada claimed his wife became addicted to liquor and drugs and that he tried to place her under the care of a physician.

A third party, Joe Uyehara, the husband's cousin, was arrested with the couple on charges of disturbing the peace. The *Laramie Republican* said that Yamada and Uyehara were released on personal recognizance, while Newman Yamada was "refused bail." The *Republican* suggested Denver law enforcement had a special relationship with Suyeki Yamada and his club, Toyo-Doshi.

The Albany County clerk's office issued another interracial marriage license in 1910. The groom was Joe Yashina, a Japanese man from Cheyenne, and the wife was Anna Albers, a white woman over the age of twenty-one. The newspaper said Joe was an intelligent-looking "Oriental" much lighter in color than some of his compatriots. The couple married in Laramie in March 1910. Joe Yashina could be Joe Yoshima, a twenty-three-year-old gambler who lived in Cheyenne during the 1910 census.

There was also an unusual wedding between a Japanese man and a young white woman in Cheyenne in June 1910. On June 20, 1910, the *Cheyenne State Leader* ran the headline "White Girl Bride of Her Jap Knight." The knight who defended a girl's honor in this soap opera of a fairy tale was Saida Inamoto. The bride was Mable Hawkins, a sixteen-year-old white girl. Both parties were from the agricultural town of Eaton, Colorado.

Two days earlier, Inamoto had pulled a knife on Sam Lopez and chased him through the streets of the Russian quarter of Eaton, known as St. Petersburg, because he made improper advances to Mable Hawkins. Each man considered Mable his sweetheart. Lopez escaped unscathed, but he pressed charges of assault and battery against Inamoto. The Japanese man was arrested, pleaded guilty and paid a fine. However, before Lopez could get out of court, authorities detained him after Hawkins accused Lopez of attempted assault. The *Cheyenne State Leader* article said Lopez sat in jail while Inamoto, Hawkins and the girl's father went to Cheyenne for a wedding.

Even though interracial marriages were legal in Wyoming for a time, not all judges performed such weddings. In 1911, Albany County District Court judge Carpenter declined to marry H. Kamido of Laramie and Bertha Oien, a white woman from Cheyenne. The following month, the judge refused to marry two young Japanese men to two white girls. The *Park County Enterprise* said, "Wyoming has at least one judge which has the right conception of the marriage vow. Yesterday two Japs appeared before Judge Carpenter and asked him to unite them to two white girls, and the judge very politely refused to do so. The judge said this thing of Japs marrying American girls is getting altogether too common, and he will not be a party to any such thing."[84]

CHAPTER 17

JAPANESE AT RED BUTTES

Red Buttes is east of Laramie and six miles from Fort Sanders, the army fort built to protect workers constructing the Transcontinental Railroad. Red Buttes was little more than a section house for westbound trains; there was very little excitement in this side station with a population of 110. In 1906, a "little Japanese section hand" discovered a broken rail just as a heavy passenger train approached at fifty miles an hour. The *Laramie Boomerang* said the "little man, never hesitated a moment as he ran as he never ran before towards the oncoming train, frantically waving his handkerchief all the while. He was seen by the engine crew and the train was stopped before the danger point was reached."[85]

Six years later, Xeshiro Moto, who was in charge of an extra gang of forty men, was arrested for selling liquor to his men. So why was Moto arrested? After all, drinking is the great American pastime. But prohibition was Union Pacific policy. Union Pacific president H.G. Burt discouraged employee drinking by closing saloons and banning drinking in company eating houses along the line in 1898. The company even discharged employees seen entering or leaving a bar, even if the employee did not drink.[86] The railroad did this to protect the lives of passengers.

In 1918, Union Pacific asked Wyoming governor Frank Houx for help closing saloons along the line from nine o'clock in the evening to seven in the morning.[87] Union Pacific Coal Company also successfully shuttered

This Japanese section crew working at Red Buttes is the only known photographic evidence of Japanese immigrants working for the Union Pacific. *Wyoming State Archives.*

a saloon in Elmo, a Swedish community outside Hanna. But Sweetwater County resisted. The worst of the coal mining communities was Rock Springs, which had more saloons than any other city.[88]

Red Buttes also had natural products of commercial importance such as gypsum, volcanic ash, bentonite and soda. Gypsum was first developed commercially in 1889 by the Red Buttes Cement and Plaster Company; the company produced thirty tons of finished product daily at capacity.[89] Consolidated Plaster Company took over operations in 1897. In its twenty-year history, CPC employed at least one Japanese worker. Torhiko Tanigawa was thirty-five years old and had lived in Laramie since 1906. He once ran the Japanese boardinghouse and pool hall on Second Street before working for CPC on the night shift. In November 1916, Tanigawa fell from the second story at the plant and died a short while later at a hospital in Laramie. Colorado Portland Cement Company bought the plant the following year and operated the plant until its closure in 1923.

CHAPTER 18

WYOMING WIND

Wyoming wind is common. Wyoming's altitude and mountains collide with the jet stream and push air to lower elevations to create the effect. Along the Union Pacific, Rawlins, Laramie and Cheyenne rank among the windiest cities in the Wyoming Division.

In 1906, twenty Japanese section workers sleeping in outfit cars were injured in the early morning of June 28 when a small tornado blew eleven Union Pacific cars from the track and destroyed a mile of telegraph line at Weir, a Union Pacific station east of Cheyenne. Seven Japanese workers were seriously hurt. They were placed on a special train and taken to hospitals in Omaha, Nebraska. Union Pacific repaired the telegraph lines, and the Japanese lived in boxcars until carpenters repaired the damaged bunks in the outfit cars.[90]

On the night of October 21, 1908, the Union Pacific Extra 224 work train derailed 1.5 miles east of Sherman. Six men died when gale-force wind hurled a caboose over the edge of a fill. The dead included two Japanese men who died when thrown through a window.

Sherman was a small town near the Ames Monument. Union Pacific built a roundhouse with five stalls, a turntable, two section houses, a windmill and a water tank here. The accident occurred around seven o'clock in the evening as the UP Extra backed from Hermosa to Buford. The Extra had just come out of Lone Tree fill when the wind lifted the caboose off the track three times. The caboose with thirty-nine men was wrenched free from the coupling and hurled over the edge of the fill, one of the highest on the Union Pacific.

Ames Monument. Two Japanese workers died at Sherman, near the Ames Monument, when a tornado blew their work train off the tracks. *Wyoming State Archives.*

Sherman Town. Sherman station had a roundhouse, section houses and a windmill with a water tank. Today, it is a ghost town. *Wyoming State Archives.*

Conductor Jim Lowery and Roadmaster William Corliss braved the gale-force winds and walked two miles in pitch darkness to Buford to report the accident. Lowery said the car "was broken into kindling wood." Conductor Lowery had worked for UP since 1888. He said this was the first time he remembered wind blowing a broad-gauge car off the track. When asked if anybody was responsible for the accident, Lowery replied, "No, sir, nobody only, I suppose, God Almighty, is the way I got it figured out, only just the wind."[91]

During the rescue, workers removed a hot stove to reach the workers pinned under the wreckage. After midnight, rescue workers placed the injured on a train bound for Cheyenne.[92] The coroner's inquest identified the two dead Japanese men as Buichi Mori and Osomu Hiromota. Both men were twenty-nine years old. Kantaro Okuda, the Japanese interpreter for Union Pacific, said Hiromota was very big for a Japanese man. He was about six feet tall, stout, fat and weighed more than 170 pounds. Mori had a more typical Japanese build. He was five feet and three or four inches tall and weighed between 130 and 135 pounds.

Both men are buried at Potter's Field in Greenhill Cemetery in Laramie.

CHAPTER 19

MURDER IN A SECTION CAMP?

Buford was important to the Union Pacific. The company invested $2,500,000 in this area of eastern Albany County to build a cutoff from Buford on the east slope of Sherman Hill to Laramie. Union Pacific completed the cutoff in February 1901. The work involved excavating "over 160,000 cubic yards per mile." To the east of Buford, Union Pacific double-tracked sixteen miles to Borie. Additionally, Buford had a quarry that supplied Union Pacific with ballast for its road between Omaha and Rock Springs, a distance of more than eight hundred miles. The quarry at Buford excavated about ten thousand carloads of ballast a year between 1902 and 1916.[93]

There was little excitement in this wayside Wyoming hamlet. Then, in March 1908, a carload of dynamite stored in an abandoned barracks at the gravel pit exploded. The explosion tore a great hole in the bottom of the gravel pit and destroyed two buildings and several hundred yards of telegraph wire.[94] The Japanese community in Buford was small enough to fit into two section houses. One section house was for Iwataro Hirata, the Japanese section foreman, and his wife. The Japanese ate together in a common cookhouse. Seichi Hiraka (also spelled Hiracka) later added a small room to the cookhouse because he did not want to live with the other section men. He was still charged eight dollars for this private room. Hiraka was forty years old, with brown hair and eyes and a dark complexion. He was also five feet tall, but an article in the *Laramie*

Bird's-eye view of Buford yards. A Japanese section worker died in a fire in 1909. A local paper said the corpse was headless and legless. *Wyoming State Archives.*

Republican suggested he was considerably shorter when he died on January 31, 1909, in a mysterious fire.

Seichi Hiraka's death was ruled accidental by the coroner's panel that convened, but I believe his death was not an accident but something more sinister. I believe this because of what the Japanese interpreter said during the inquest and what was reported in the *Laramie Boomerang*.

The following information was obtained from the coroner's inquest on file at the Wyoming State Archives in Cheyenne. Shortly after midnight on January 31, section foreman Iwataro Hirata noticed a structure fire at the cookhouse where Hiraka lived. Iwataro was born in Japan in 1874 and immigrated to the United States in 1893. He also spoke English. The coroner's panel, however, swore Kantaro Okuda in as an interpreter because he was the Union Pacific's Japanese interpreter for Wyoming's Fifth and Sixth Districts. Moreover, Okuda spoke English quite well, said the local newspaper. The following is a reprint of the questions asked at the coroner's inquest. The excerpt is essential because Okuda gives insight into the victim's character.

University of Wyoming campus. Kantaro Okuda, Union Pacific's interpreter for the Fifth and Sixth Districts, graduated from UW in 1911 with bachelor's and master's degrees. *Wyoming State Archives.*

Coroner's panel questions for Kantaro Okuda:

> *Q: Where do you work?*
> *A. Buford, Wyo.*
>
> *Q: Who for?*
> *A: U.P. Railroad Company*
>
> *Q: Do you know the man whose body is lying here, the body of the man we just looked at?*
> *A: Yes.*
>
> *Q: What is his name?*
> *A: Seichi Hiracka.*

Q: Did he work for the U.P.?
A: Yes, sir.

Q: How long have you worked with him at Buford?
A: Two months.

Q: Tell what you know about how the man met his death?
A: Burned up.

Q: State your name?
A: K. Okuda.

Q: Where do you live?
A: Cheyenne.

Q: What business?
A: Working for U.P. Interpreter.

Q: Were you acquainted with this man who is lying dead here?
A: Yes.

Q: Are you acquainted with the Buford pits?
A: Yes.

Q: Tell us the facts in relation to this man's death?
A: The house which was burned on the first of this month was used for a cooking house. This man built a small house by the cooking house for his sleeping room. Buford section has one bunkhouse for section laborers, but it is not big enough for the section force, so just himself occupied that small shanty. At 12:30 on the first of this month the section foreman noticed this fire, he went to the shanty and tried to open the door, after he opened it, he found out that all inside the room was full of flame, so he could get in, the foreman couldn't take him out.

Q: Have you any idea how the fire started?
A: In my opinion the fire started from the heating stove which was placed in the shanty.

Q: Do you know whether there had been any trouble among the Japanese section men?
A: No, I don't think there was any trouble between anybody there.

Q: In your opinion this fire just occurred from the stove and the man smothered to death?
A: The heating stove was put by the door so I believe he could not come out through the door. That door was on fire first.

Q: Where was the remains found, on the bed?
A: After everything burned the remains were found on the iron bed on the spring. I didn't witness it, but understand this from the statement of the section man.

Q: Do you know whether this man had any money or property?
A: I want to explain what kind of man he was. He was a man who never paid any attention to money, never tried to save money, his habit was gambling some time. He didn't save any money, I don't think. I understand that he never received a letter from home or ever sent one there. He has been away from home [a] long time. He was [a] seaman when he came over here.

He was a kind of bad character.

I don't believe he had money. I was acquainted with him for [a] long time. He gambled in Cheyenne and Ogden several months ago, I didn't hear anything that he gambled at Buford.

The jury determined the deceased was smothered and burned in a structure fire without awakening. How was he smothered? What makes this death even more suspicious is that the *Laramie Republican* reported, "The headless and legless trunk of the man will be brought to this city and an inquest held."[95] When I shared this story with my good friend Wayne, a retired firefighter, he raised an eyebrow. What happened to Hiraka's head and legs? The Japanese interpreter said Hiraka was a "bad man" and a gambler. This makes me wonder if his death was a mob gang-type hit.

PART VI

JAPANESE IN LARAMIE COUNTY

Laramie County is the last of the five original Wyoming counties to get Japanese immigrant labor.

Before the 1900 census, there was only 1 Japanese person living in Laramie County. He was K. Ogita, who was born in Japan in 1872 and immigrated at fourteen years old. He worked as a cook. He could speak, read and write in English. Although many Japanese came to Wyoming in the early 1900s, Japanese immigrants did not appear on the Cheyenne census because they arrived after the census. However, the earliest documentation of their presence was in 1905. The Japanese population in Cheyenne that year was somewhere between 30 and 35. In all of Laramie County, there were 117 Japanese people.

In March 1905, the *Wyoming Tribune* announced that approximately five hundred Japanese laborers would arrive in the capital city over the next two months. The Wakimoto-Nishimura Japanese employment agency said the men would be distributed on the sections of the Nebraska Division from North Platte to Omaha and between Cheyenne and Denver.[96] In late April, a "Jap Army" of one hundred laborers arrived from San Francisco and were sent to Denver for work on various sections of the Union Pacific in Colorado and on the Cheyenne-Denver branch. The *Cheyenne Daily Leader* said they attracted considerable attention on the streets that morning.[97]

By 1910, there were 417 Japanese in Cheyenne and the Laramie County communities of Archer, Arcola, Badger, Bordeaux, Borie, Campstool, Chugwater, Fish Creek, Granite Canyon, Hartville, Hazard, Horse Creek, Otto, Pine Bluffs,

Sunrise, Wyncote and the army post at Fort D.A. Russell. In May 1911, Union Pacific graders and laborers double-tracked the road between Pine Bluffs, Wyoming, and Julesburg, Colorado. UP rebuilt the yards at Pine Bluffs and moved the depot to the stockyards and the stockyards to the north side of the tracks opposite the elevator. The old section house moved off the right of way, and the water tank and pumping station relocated near the coal chutes.[98]

CHAPTER 20

CHEYENNE'S JAPAN TOWNS

C heyenne had two Japanese towns. North Japan Town was in the heart of Cheyenne. This Japan Town stretched between Fifteenth and Twenty-Fourth Streets and from Russell Avenue to Bent Avenue. The 1910 census shows several Japanese people also worked and lived at St. John's Hospital. The majority of Japanese lived between Fifteenth and Seventeenth Streets and Carey Avenue and Bent Avenue. There were several boardinghouses in the northern section, a Japanese hospital, a couple of restaurants, a barbershop, a pool hall, Okano's photo studio and the Cheyenne Trading Company Wholesale and Retail Store run by George Wakimoto. Today, there is only one building in Cheyenne associated with Japan Town. According to census records, the building at 311 West Sixteenth Street was a former Japanese boardinghouse and a Chinese-owned restaurant called Bon Ton.

Cheyenne's second Japanese town was south of the Union Pacific roundhouse. It was near Crow Creek, in a section the locals called "the bottoms." The Japanese lived in C&S bunk cars on railroad property and company-owned houses between the one hundred and seven hundred blocks of Tenth, Eleventh and Twelfth Streets.

This section flooded on May 1904. On the evening of the flood, inhabitants living near a hill parallel to the Colorado and Southern tracks rushed to safety as the torrents of the Crow Creek destroyed fences, bridges and homes; the storm also cut off telegraphic communication[99] and washed

According to census records, the second building from the right is the only Japanese boardinghouse left in Cheyenne. It was also Bon Ton, a Chinese-owned restaurant. *Author's collection.*

Cheyenne's second Japan Town was south of the roundhouse. Japanese lived in C&S bunk cars and in company section housing. *Wyoming State Archives.*

away the gravel ballast underneath Union Pacific tracks along an eight- to ten-mile stretch between Buford and Cheyenne.[100]

This southern Japanese town existed until 1935, when Union Pacific extended its Cheyenne shop farther south, and in the process, section housing was demolished. By then, many Japanese people living in Cheyenne started to return to Japan.

CHAPTER 21

SHOOTOUT IN CHEYENNE

T he Wakimoto-Nishimura Japanese agency had an office in North Japan Town, on Fifteenth Street, near the Union Pacific depot. Unfortunately for the generally genial George Wakimoto, someone tried to "shoot the ears off" him as he walked to work on April 7, 1904. The trouble stemmed from an incident the morning before, when Wakimoto demanded Thomas Yoshihara pay up on a $20 loan (almost $667 in 2023). The local paper said Wakimoto then proceeded to "beat him up in true American style." Yoshihara escaped with a black eye and numerous bruises.

Yoshihara was a railroad laborer with a side hustle as a gambler. The *Wyoming Tribune* alleged Yoshihara had ties to a powerful Japanese secret society, similar to the Highbinder Tongs of the Chinese, and that he operated illegal gambling games among the Japanese section gangs. After his beating, Yoshihara later purchased a .38-caliber revolver from a secondhand store.[101] He confronted Wakimoto and fired five shots.

One bullet crashed through the window of the nearby Moran restaurant. The second projectile narrowly missed the young lady cashier at Kabis restaurant. The third round hit the restaurant building. A fourth bullet that "whistled by" Wakimoto's head hit the Union Pacific depot. Yoshihara fired a fifth round at Wakimoto as he ran west on Fifteenth Street toward the Japanese hospital and boardinghouse.

Cheyenne law enforcement charged Thomas Yoshihara with assault with intent to kill. The penalty for this offense was one to fourteen years at the state penitentiary in Rawlins.[102] Out of curiosity, I returned to the crime

Left: A Cheyenne gambler tried to "shoot the ears off" the Japanese labor agent. He missed, and the bullet lodged in the train depot wall. *Author's collection.*

Below: Train depot and café. A shootout in Japan Town occurred in 1904 at the Union Pacific train depot. Japanese agent George Wakimoto was shaken but unharmed. *Author's collection.*

scene to see if I could find the bullet or the impact area on the depot. I found a hole in the white sandstone west of the entrance of the train depot. Someone repaired the damaged area with a similar sandstone material, but I could still make out the bullet's circular shape, and now I wonder, is the bullet still lodged in the wall?

CHAPTER 22

JAP GAMBLING CLUB RAIDED

O n August 1910, Cheyenne police raided an illegal Japanese gambling club and arrested thirty-one men at a billiard hall near the Salvation Army headquarters. Police learned of the illicit operation after a Japanese man they arrested told them about a secret room at 423 West Seventeenth Street. Cheyenne police had long suspected the Japanese had a gambling den, but they could never find it because there was a remote buzzer system at the front of the hall to tip off the gamblers about a police raid.

Police battered down the rear door of the pool hall with a six-by-six piece of lumber and found hundreds of dollars on the tables, a large sack of money, Japanese markers, four hundred packs of cards, various gambling paraphernalia, hunting knives, dirks, revolvers and men playing poker, dice games and fan-fan. Many Japanese gamblers had large sums of money in their pockets, including a man by the surname of Matseyama. He had more than $1,000 on his person, which is the 2022 equivalent of more than $28,000. However, one man lost much of his cash winnings when he tripped and spilled a bulging pocketful of silver coins after a police officer tried to shoot him as he fled.

Twenty of the men arrested were bonded out by "Little Joe," a proprietor of a Japanese store. Little Joe was not in favor of gambling, but he paid $525 in bonds because "they were working Japs who had duties to perform about the city." The other ten men were left behind bars because "they made it a practice to gamble."[103]

CHAPTER 23

JAPANESE PLOT AT LAKEVIEW CEMETERY

L akeview Cemetery (formerly City Cemetery) was founded in 1875 after Cheyenne closed the original cemetery in west Cheyenne. Because of their poverty, many of the first generations of Japanese in Cheyenne are buried in unmarked graves in Potter's Field. When a Japanese immigrant died, they were laid to rest with the charitable help of the local Japanese population or with the assistance of the city or attending mortuary.

In the case of a deceased who left behind any assets, his estate paid for the services and the $5 interment fee, and the balance was dispersed to survivors. S. Yamamoto was one of those who left behind an estate. He died when a locomotive hit him. He left a $1 Ingersoll watch and $9.90 in cash. A death certificate was also issued, but generally, there was little or no mention of the death. With the help of Robin Everett at the Wyoming State Archives and resource books in the Cheyenne Genealogical Collection at the Laramie County Library in Cheyenne, I compiled a spreadsheet of the early Japanese immigrants buried in Potter's Field and a section called the Japanese plot.

Approximately fifty-seven Japanese people were interred in Potter's Field during the first decades of the twentieth century. The first Japanese person buried at Lakeview was twenty-seven-year-old C. Nakashima. He perished in a snowstorm on April 19, 1905. Less than a week later, I. Inouye, a section hand, died from what the *Wyoming Tribune* described as a "comparatively unimportant injury." Inouye died from blood poisoning after a train hit him

Many headstones in the Japanese plot at Lakeview Cemetery have Japanese and English writing. Several monuments also have Christian symbols. *Author's collection.*

and broke his arm; he spent six weeks at St. John's Hospital in Cheyenne before passing.[104] One of the more unusual deaths is that of Susho Watiari. He was found dead outside St. John's Hospital after he sustained injuries in an automobile accident in Kimball, Nebraska. Kimball is sixty miles from Cheyenne. On April 13, 1911, Wyoming roadmaster William Corliss and his Japanese passenger, Susho Watiari, collided with a train. Corliss said the train was about a quarter mile down the track before he attempted the crossing. Corliss also told the coroner's panel several times that his vision was obstructed by a dust storm as he made the attempt and that the "Jap" had his head down. Neither Corliss nor his passenger saw or heard the approaching train. Corliss sustained a head injury, but Watiari had a fractured skull, broken ribs and a broken arm. Union Pacific personnel treated the injured men at the station, and a special train with a medical staff shuttled the men to Cheyenne, where Watiari died. No blame was assigned, and Watiari's death was ruled an automobile accident.

Slightly to the north of Potter's Field is the Japanese plot. There are thirty-three time-worn grave markers here in Section 6. Local historians are unsure why the Japanese plot came to be, but I believe there is a connection between the founding of the Japanese plot in 1924 and the passage of the Immigration Act of 1924 (also known as the Johnson-Reid Act). The Immigration Act ended further Japanese immigration, so the Japanese needed a landmark to remember their dead. Some of the bodies were exhumed and shipped to Denver for cremation.

Many headstones in the Japanese plot have Japanese characters, English or both languages engraved. In addition, there are many headstones with Christian symbols; this illustrates the Japanese people's willingness to assimilate into Western culture. The Christian symbols on the headstones are a reflection of the Methodist Church's attempt in late August 1905 to convert "Japs" and Scandinavians in Wyoming. The Baptist Church in Cheyenne also ministered to the Japanese community through an Americanization program in 1924. However, the Japanese were introduced to the teachings of Jesus Christ as early as 1549. Many of the markers in the Japanese plot tell a story of Japanese adoption of Christianity. The mission to evangelize and assimilate the Japanese appeared successful, because many memorials have Christian symbols such as a cross, dove, lamb or carving of lilies of the valley.[105] Pictures of Japanese funerals on file at the Wyoming State Archives also reflect that the graveside burial ceremony was often Christian in nature.

The following is a list of the Japanese buried in Potter's Field, the Japanese plot and the newborn plot. I found this information in the City Cemetery Tombstone and Cemetery Records, 1875–1910; the Laramie County coroner's reports; and the Wyoming State Archives Death Certificate online database at wyospcr.state.wy.us.

Author notes: an asterisk (*) beside the name means the person has a Japanese headstone but is not Japanese. A double asterisk (**) means the person is buried outside the Japanese plot.

Last Name	First Name	Died	Month	Day	Age	Cause of Death
Arai	Mine	1926	Nov.	15	32	Train accident
Aresumio	Rihaichiro	1915	Sept.	2	31	Accident
Demozco	Leki	1922	Aug.	15	65	Uremia
Demozco	(Son)	1921	Feb.	23	3d	Malformation/ inanition
Ettie	Taito	1912	May	23	2	Accidental suffocation
Fukayawa	K.	1932	Dec.	17	61	Abdominal aneurysm
Fukushima**	Mae Tome	1923	Apr.	27	48	Lysol poisoning

LAST NAME	FIRST NAME	DIED	MONTH	DAY	AGE	CAUSE OF DEATH
Fukuyawa	F.	1932	Dec.	19	61	Abdominal aneurysm
Futa	S. (son)	1916	Jan.	14	3d	Dystocia of mother
Hakama	Child	1908	Sept.	28	5	Uremia
Hakoma	Child	1908	Sept.	28	5	
Hamada	Vizi	1907	Jan.	27	26	Train accident
Hara	Masao	1913	Sept.	19	8d	Premature birth
Hayashi	Y. (daughter)	1915	Jan.	30		Inanition
Hirata	Kimey	1910	July	4	9m	Pneumonia
Ibata	Masa	1931	Jan.	20	45	Diabetic coma
Ibata	Unsabe	1925	Sept.	25	51	Carcinoma of stomach
Ichimatsu	Kirose	1918	Mar.	22	36	Pharyngeal abscess
Inaoki	Moto (son)	1916	Sept.	26		Transverse presentation
Inouya	I.	1905	Apr.	25		Blood poisoning
Ito	S.	1910	July	13	23	Tuberculosis
Iwanoto	Inohichio	1908	Apr.	15		
Iwasaki	Hajime	1917	June	4	2m 24d	Meningitis
Kagawa	Kenjiro	1928	Oct.	8	45	Pneumonia
Kamatsa	M.	1912	Feb.	11		UPRR yard accident
Kamatsu	Wanasuhi	1912	Dec.	12	44	RR yard accident
Kamidoi	Harry	1912	Jan.	31		Premature birth
Kanji (Kanja)	S.	1908	Nov.	13	28	RR accident
Katsumato	Y.	1909	Nov.	10	26	Typhoid fever
Kawagishi	S.	1908	Apr.	15	25	Typhoid fever
Kawaguchi	Kazuto (Bob)	1946	Jan.	17	1y 25d	Pneumonia
Kawaguehige	(daughter)	1942	Sept.	23		Premature birth
Koza	G. (daughter)	1916	Oct.	10	1d	Syphilis
Kubota	H. (K.)	1908	Nov.	13	38	RR accident
Kuga	(son)	1928	Dec.	7		Premature birth

Last Name	First Name	Died	Month	Day	Age	Cause of Death
Kuga	Zini (son)	1928	Mar.	22	1m	Pneumonia
Kurahashi	Toijiro					No info available
Mammamoto	Kinnosuka	1908	Mar.	3		Pneumonia
Masunaga	Suchiko	1931	July	14	44	Uremia
Matsuishima	Kiku	1927	Feb.	28	42	Eclampsia
Matsuishima	Takimatsu	1944	July	24	63	Accidental fall
Mimami	T.	1906	Aug.	19		C&W RR yard accident
Mimamoto	Kimosuke	1908	Mar.	2		Heart disease
Mizakuni	K.	1905	Sept.	9	26	RR cars
Mumamoto	Kinnosuke	1908	Mar.	3	33	Pneumonia
Nakaba	Keisabura	1942	May	9	43	Stomach cancer
Nakagowa*	Sadie	1911	May	8	28	Killed by husband
Nakamoto	T.	1914	Aug.	10	32	Nasal hemorrhage
Nakano	Hina	1923	Sept.	23	23	Tuberculosis
Nakashima	C.	1905	Apr.	22	27	Snowstorm
Nakashima	Saburo	1921	Oct.	24	44	Uremia
Nishijima	Tameki	1924	Feb.	6	41	Heart attack
Nishimura	Rikuma	1915	Mar.	8	30	Accident
Obata	Fusakuha	1924	Sept.	23	44	Tuberculosis
Ogasawara	Tsumasaburo	1938	Jan.	3	/4	Arteriosclerosis
Ogihara	Frederick	1923	Mar.	6	6d	Liver atrophy
Ohito	M.	1907	June	27	41	RR accident
Oki	M.	1915	Mar.	1	17	Pneumonia
Okinnora	K.	1906	Sept.	6	39	
Okomoto	H	1908	Nov.	13	39	RR accident
Okumora	K.	1906	Sept.	6	39	Typhoid fever
Ono	Kamensuki	1912	Dec.	11	25	Peritonitis
Saito	Ettie	1912	May	23	2m	Accidental suffocation
Saito	Shikashi	1918	Dec.	11	22	Fractured skull
Sakamoto	Eikichi	1915	Nov.	20	42	Accident
Sakamoto	George					No info available

Last Name	First Name	Died	Month	Day	Age	Cause of Death
Sakuma	Kenji					No death certificate
Sakuma	Minor					No death certificate
Sakuma	Tomo	1912				Shared grave with Kenji
Satow	Kimo	1918	Feb.	17	35	Eclampsia
Seino	K.	1925	June	29	45	Cerebral hemorrhage
Sen	Soon	1923	July	17	60	Pulmonary oedemia
Sonoda	Heitaro	1916	Nov.	5	31	Strangulation
Tabahe	Joshinatsu	1907	June	1	22	RR accident
Takamoto	E.	1915	Nov.	20		UPRR yard accident
Takano	Kima	1926	June	17	27	Meningitis
Takimobu	U.	1919	June	19	54	Carcinoma
Tanabe	Joshnatsu	1907	June	13	22	RR accident
Tanaka	M.	1913	May	4		Gunshot wound
Tanoka	Matsutore	1913	May	6	35	Gunshot wound
Tanuba	Y.	1907	June			Train accident
Terao	Edward	1932	Aug.	24	4m	Pneumonia
Tokimobu	U.	1919	June	21	54	Carcinoma
Tom	Charles	1919	Jan.	10	67	Tuberculosis
Tom	Kim	1918	Oct.	12	38	Cardiac insufficiency
Toyota	Yenmi	1907	Jan.	23	24	Meningitis
Toyoto	Yenj	1907	Nov.	11	24	
Uyehara*	Cora King	1918	April	18	33	Buried outside Section 6
Watairi	Susho	1911	April	13		Auto accident
Yaeko	Suzuki	1923	March	19	4	Tuberculosis/ meningitis
Yama	Taru	1914	Jan.	23	30	Peritonitis

Last Name	First Name	Died	Month	Day	Age	Cause of Death
Yamada	Taroichi	1911	Dec.	15	39	Appendicitis
Yamamoto	I.	1911	July	30	45	RR accident
Yamamoto	S.	1911	July	29		Train accident
Yamamoto	(son)	1921	Feb.	23	3d	Malformation/ inanition
Yamamoto	Toshika	1926	Jan.	9	6m	Pneumonia
Yamamoto	(son)	1930	Aug.	13	8d	Premature birth
Yashe	J.	1924	May	18	38	Meningitis
Yoshimaru	Seikichi	1949	Mar.	3	75	Myocarditis
Yoshimaru	Sumiye	1917	Feb.	16	30	Mitral regurgitation

CHAPTER 24

RAILROAD SAFETY CONTESTS

Many of the Japanese buried in the Japanese plot and Potter's Field were killed in railroad accidents. As a result, the Union Pacific improved its safety measures to protect its workers, and the company even set a safety standard benchmark in 1923 of only five casualties per million man-hours worked. Other railway companies followed Union Pacific and copied its safety model. However, I found it disturbing that some division superintendents creatively reported accidents and deaths when "the game was tight." For example, J.V. Anderson, a former superintendent of the Wyoming Division, insisted a "Japanese boy" died of natural causes from heart failure when he discovered a train bearing down on him just before it struck him.[106]

George H. Warfel, an assistant to the general manager in charge of safety in the Omaha Division, wrote an article for *Union Pacific Magazine* in 1931. Warfel said that superintendents received demerits for accidents in their division. He gave an example when a Colorado Division fireman jumped from a moving train to retrieve a coffee pot as the train climbed the Sherman Hill grade. The fireman broke his arm when he jumped back onto the train as it crossed into the Wyoming Division. Warfel said, "Men over the road still smile" over the definitive answer a roadmaster gave when asked if he wasn't constantly worried that one of his men would get killed. The roadmaster replied, "If he does, I'll take him out by the right-of-way fence and bury him and say nothing about it until our division has won this contest."

Many of the Japanese buried in Lakeview Cemetery who died in railroad-related accidents were often blamed as being the cause of the accident. In the case of the Japanese or other non-English-speaking immigrants, the standard excuse was the victim did not understand English. In January 1907, Thomas Hamada died in a C&S train accident at Bourdeaux. Hamada was unloading cars with an extra gang when an engine approached to move the freight cars. The *Wyoming Tribune* said Hamada heard the foreman call for the men to get off the train, but he just smiled at the foreman, turned and went back to work.[107]

The engine bumped the car, knocking Hamada to his death under the wheels. The *Wyoming Tribune* said his death "was attributed to the fact that he could not understand the English language." However, if it were true that Hamada didn't understand English, he indeed would have understood the wild gesticulation of the foreman telling all workers to get off the train. An inquest by Coroner T.C. Murray found Hamada's death was due to an accident, and the company was not held responsible.[108]

CHAPTER 25

RUNAWAY TRAIN

AT BORIE STATION

A train accident at Borie Station, west of Cheyenne, on November 10, 1908, killed nine men. One newspaper said the dead included "six railroad men and three Japanese victims." The Japanese were S. Kanja (twenty-eight), K. Kubota (thirty-eight) and H. Okamoto. Two men had wives back in Japan. Kubota's remains were exhumed in 1926, and relatives sent his body to Denver for cremation. The *Cheyenne Daily Leader* said the Borie wreck was the worst in the Wyoming Division. It was also the first time in its history that a train from the Wyoming Division collided with a train from the Colorado Division.[109]

Three railway officials and two civilians composed the coroner's inquest board. They said the air brakes on the Union Pacific freight train malfunctioned before leaving Laramie for its run over Sherman Hill.[110] The train had insufficient air pressure in its brake lines to force the brake shoe against the wheel to slow the train during its descent of Sherman Hill. Because of the brake failure, the engineer couldn't make the required scheduled stops every five minutes to allow the wheels and brakes time to cool. The train "got beyond control of the brakes" as a result of the extreme cold and frosted rails. An operator telegraphed Cheyenne when the train missed its stop at Granite Canyon. It gained momentum as it ran downhill for nine miles. Union Pacific officials intended to clear the rail yards and give the speeding train an open track through Cheyenne to Archer Hill, where they hoped the train would lose momentum. Tragically, the runaway train

Borie train wreck. A runaway train lost its air brakes and slammed into a Japanese work train in 1908. Three Japanese people died in the fiery wreck. *Wyoming State Archives.*

rear-ended a Japanese work train just as it rolled onto the main line from the Athol-Borie cut-off.

Thirty cars piled into a great heap of wreckage two hundred feet long and forty feet high and immediately caught fire. One hundred railway employees and a squad of firemen from Cheyenne battled the coal- and lumber-fueled blaze for twenty-four hours before it was contained.

CHAPTER 26

THE MURDER

OF SADIE NAKAGOWA

The Japanese plot has many marble and sandstone tributes etched with beautiful Japanese writing. However, not everyone here who has a memorial written in Japanese is Japanese. For example, there is a grave in the northwest corner of the Japanese plot of a white woman named Sadie Nakagowa (also spelled Nakagawa). If you have a smartphone with a translation app, the faded characters on her headstone will tell you she was murdered by her jealous Japanese husband in May 1911.

Sadie and Frank Nakagowa met in Colorado in 1905 and married that same year. Sadie had been married once before and had received a handsome divorce settlement. She also had a nine-year-old daughter, Frannie, who lived with Sadie's parents in Rochester, New York. The *Tribune-Stockman-Farmer*, one of the Wyoming newspapers that reported Sadie's murder, seemed obsessed with Sadie's wealth. The newspaper said that she "seemed always to have plenty of money." The tabloid emphasized her silk dress and diamonds on her fingers and in her ears. It also mentioned a small chamois bag of diamonds she had about her neck when she died.

However, Sadie did not live a fairy tale princess life. Frank was a "handsome chap," but he was more of a fractured fairy tale prince than a knight in shining armor. Frank was five-foot-three, and he was a "natty dresser" and had one upper gold tooth. He was also ten years Sadie's junior. Frank was a successful gambler who conducted a "Jap Club" in Denver, Colorado, but the couple moved often because of Frank's job. The couple had lived in Laramie, but Frank was arrested for operating an illegal gambling joint, and

Sadie Nakagowa's headstone. Sadie was a white woman. Her Japanese husband murdered her in a boardinghouse. He was never caught. *Author's collection.*

Laramie city officials ran the couple out of town. So, the couple settled in Cheyenne.

Neighbors and friends who knew the couple said they fought often. Frank was jealous whenever one of his fellow citizens cast an eye toward Sadie, but he didn't hesitate to use his good looks and charm to his advantage. Shortly before the murder, Frank struck up a relationship with Babe Murphy, a resident of a red-light district resort in west Cheyenne. Sadie later discovered a letter from Babe Murphy after she returned from visiting family in New York. Sadie confronted Frank about the letter and asked for a divorce. Frank, in a fit of anger, stabbed Sadie in the neck at a "Jap Boarding House" at 514 West Seventeenth Street.

Frank Nakagowa fled into the night wearing a dark suit, a dark red sweater with a tiny stripe and a light-colored Stetson hat. The local newspaper, however, speculated he would try to flee the city "dressed as a woman." Laramie County also offered $250 reward for the arrest of the jealous Japanese murderer, Frank Nakagowa.

Within five minutes after the report of the killing had been received at police headquarters, Chief Schoel had detailed every available man on the force to different sections of the city and the railroad yards to keep a close lookout for the fleeing fugitive. The police searched every resort frequented by the Japanese. A credible witness reported a foreigner on the wagon road leading to Denver. This prompted law enforcement to search every ranch house between Cheyenne and Carr, Colorado, for the elusive Frank Nakagowa.[111]

Railroad switchmen also spotted him in Laramie, but they did not try to apprehend him. Law enforcement believed Nakagowa was headed to Green River, where his brother lived. A train crew saw Frank Nakagowa on a westbound train, but once again, no one tried to apprehend him. The last reported sighting of Frank Nakagowa was in Ogden, Utah.

Just west of the Japanese plot is the grave of Cora King Uyehara. She was also white, and a Japanese headstone marks her final resting place. Cora and her husband, Joe, were married for seven years and operated a chicken ranch on Happy Jack Road. Joe also had ties to the Toyo-Doshi Japanese club in Denver. His cousin Suyeki Yamada operated the club, and he was the Japanese man who married a white woman, Carrie Newman, in Laramie in 1910. Cora died in April 1918 after a bout with depression and addiction.

CHAPTER 27

JAPANESE AMERICANIZATION

I n addition to evangelizing the Japanese, Wyoming also tried to Americanize the Japanese even though they were ineligible for citizenship. Sometime around World War I, Wyoming appropriated nearly $5,000 a year to start a program to Americanize resident aliens.[112] The state established Americanization programs in four mining camps near Kemmerer sponsored by the local labor council and the United Mine Workers of America.[113] The General Federation of Women's Clubs also adopted an Americanization plan for the cultural exchange of music, art and food.[114]

Locally, the Women's Ministry at the First Baptist Church in Cheyenne started an Americanization program in 1924 to share the gospel of Jesus Christ and to teach American ideals and living skills to the women of Cheyenne's Japanese community. Suzi Taylor, one of the reference archivists at the Wyoming State Archives, called me about a diary she found written by Mary Julia Moore Allyn, the founder of the First Baptist Church Americanization program.

Mary Allyn was inspired to start an Americanization program after a Japanese man with two little girls knocked on her door in December 1922. He said his wife was sick. The Cheyenne Children's Home had sent him to the Allyn household because there was no room at the home for his daughters. He asked if Mrs. Allyn would care for the children until his wife got well. Allyn hesitated. She had cared for some children sent by the home, but she never had Japanese children placed under her care. Finally, she

Left: The First Baptist Church started an Americanization program after the Cheyenne Children's Home turned away caring for two young Japanese girls. *Wyoming State Archives*.

Below: Americanization teachers. Mary Allyn (*left*) started the Americanization program at First Baptist Church. Zennia Emerson (*black hat*) was the wife of Governor Frank Emerson. *Wyoming State Archives*.

asked if the man wanted the children to attend American Sunday school. Yes, he replied. He said he and his wife were Christians and wished for them to attend Sunday school.

The children stayed with the Allyns for nine months, and then the father took them to the home of a Japanese woman returning to Japan. Unfortunately, his wife, Hina Nakano, died of pulmonary tuberculosis on September 23, 1923. She was twenty-three. Before she died, she said she was going to Jesus and asked her husband to sing a hymn. He sang "Nearer My God to Thee." At her services at the First Baptist Church, there was no suggestion of Japanese customs. She was buried in Potter's Field, and Mr. Nakano returned to Japan with his children a few weeks later.

The Americanization program met in various locations throughout the city, usually in the home of one of the Japanese women, in a vacant school classroom or at the church. The class topics ranged from English as a second language to how to cook American-style meals. The cooking classes were very popular. For example, one of the first classes was making lemon pie. The Japanese women diligently wrote down the recipe after sampling the pie, and then they made the pie for their families. The family of one eager woman ate lemon pie for three consecutive days.

One of the teachers in the Americanization program was Zennia Jean Reynders Emerson. Her husband, Frank, was the Wyoming governor. One day, a Japanese woman asked Zennia why the governor wasn't in church. Zennia explained Governor Emerson was working with the Wyoming legislature. She then invited the Japanese woman to visit the capitol to watch the legislative session. Zennia also arranged a party at the Governor's Mansion, which forty Japanese people attended.

The Americanization program ran into difficulties after Congress passed the Immigration Act of 1924. Coded language in the Johnson-Reid Act ruled the Japanese were "aliens ineligible for citizenship," and therefore, they were ineligible to receive Americanization study books. However, the Baptist Church continued to minister to the Japanese community until 1935, when several families in the program returned home to have their children educated in the Japanese public school system. By 1941, many of the women and children had returned to Japan.

CHAPTER 28

CHEYENNE PUBLIC SCHOOLS

Another way the Japanese assimilated into society was by sending their children to public schools when states such as California advocated for school segregation. California believed "evil consequences [were] liable to result therefrom through the indiscriminate association of our children with those of the Mongolian race."[115] Iwao Fukushima and his sister Mineko are two Japanese students who attended local public schools. The Fukushima family moved to Cheyenne in 1904. Their father, Genzo Fukushima, was a merchant and interpreter for the Union Pacific Railroad. Iwao and Mineko attended Cheyenne High. Mineko was cute, faithful, well-liked by everyone, studious and an honor student. The *Lariat* yearbook from 1917 said that she made wonderful progress in educating herself in the English language and in American customs.

Iwao was a stereotypical Japanese egghead. The *Lariat* said he would revolutionize the study of physics with his theories. He always wore a smile, and he had a "get-it-or-bust" spirit. Iwao often competed in motorcycle races and was mischievous. The fun-loving Iwao and his friends would sneak out late at night and shoot the bell on the school administration building. This led many people who heard the bell ring at midnight to believe there was a ghost in the bell tower.

After graduation, Iwao attended Colorado College in Colorado Springs, where he studied education. He also enrolled in the school's ROTC program and applied for the draft during World War I. After college, Iwao received a

Left: Mineko Fukushima graduated high school when other states practiced segregation. She made wonderful progress educating herself in the English language and American customs. *From the* Lariat *yearbook.*

Right: Iwao Fukushima taught at Dartmouth College and the University of Minnesota. He later returned to Wyoming to work for Union Pacific. *From the* Lariat *yearbook.*

teaching fellowship at Dartmouth College. He also taught at the University of Minnesota from 1920 to 1928. Iwao returned to Wyoming in 1928 and worked as a maintenance of way foreman for the Union Pacific at Harper, Wyoming. He also had a pool hall in Laramie. In March 1929, Iwao wrote an article for the *Union Pacific Magazine* titled "A Little Journey to Japan." In it, Iwao took readers on a tour through Japanese gardens and cities and the picturesque and famous Mount Fujiyama. He told readers, "English is spoken by many [Japanese], and everywhere there are signs in English." Iwao said the Japanese knew the history of the Union Pacific brand, and many former employees of the Union Pacific established themselves in education and commercial fields.

Iwao Fukushima died in 1937. His grave is outside the Japanese plot.

CHAPTER 29

COLORADO FUEL AND IRON

C olorado Fuel and Iron (CF&I) was a coal and steel company that operated iron mines in Sunrise, Wyoming. Before CF&I started harvesting the riches, the earliest iron ore miners in the area were Native American tribes such as the Sioux, Cheyenne and Arapaho, who mined the soft hematite iron ore for war paints and left behind arrowheads and stone hammers. White prospectors came to the area in 1882 to mine iron, copper, onyx, agate, gold and silver. In 1899, CF&I purchased the iron mines and adjacent mining properties for $500,000. By 1903, John D. Rockefeller had bought the company, and the local mine did business as Sunrise Iron Ore Mine; the mines at Sunrise was a wise investment for Rockefeller, as it produced 75 percent of Colorado Fuel and Iron Company's iron ore. The company initially employed seventy-five Italians, fifty-five Americans, thirty-four Greeks, fourteen Irish, nine Germans, eight French, five Austrians, four Swedes and one Scottish worker in its mines, and another fifty-two men worked for the Colorado and Wyoming Railway Company, which shipped the ore to smelters in Denver and Pueblo, Colorado.

In 1905, twenty-five Japanese people worked for the Colorado and Wyoming Railway Company, adding to Sunrise's diversity. Three years later, T. Nimami, a Japanese man employed in an extra gang for the Colorado and Wyoming Railroad at Sunrise, became the first Japanese casualty at Sunrise. He died when a heavily loaded freight car ran over his neck. The *Wyoming Tribune* said Nimami's death was peculiar because "ordinarily, a man's head would have been completely decapitated under the weight of a loaded car." Nimami's skin, however, showed no trauma.

The deceased was employed at the Sunrise mines unloading timber from cars. At the time of his death, Nimami was "in the act of setting the brake on the car with a stick, when the stick broke, and he was precipitated to the ground in front of the moving car. The wheels passing over his back, breaking the spinal column." It is unclear what became of Nimami's body.

CF&I added thirty-one Japanese residents in 1910. They worked in the iron mines and lived in a boardinghouse built to accommodate ninety-two men. Some places in Sunrise had indoor plumbing; others had hydrants near the door. Another inconvenience of living in town was when the company drilled holes and loaded them with dynamite. When the dynamite exploded, iron ore rained down and perforated roofs.[116]

Other towns in the area associated with CF&I are Hartville, Guernsey and Wheatland. After discovering gold and iron ore, CF&I also investigated expanding its operation to a one-hundred-acre parcel near Deer Creek by the Albany-Natrona County line.

Sunrise was a company town, but it was not a union town. Colorado Fuel and Iron opposed the United Mine Workers of America (UMWA). In 1903 and 1913, CF&I led the entire western coal industry in protesting the UMWA when it tried to unionize the Colorado coalfields during strikes. John D. Rockefeller Jr. once said keeping labor unions out was worth it, even "if it costs all your property and kills all your employees." Unfortunately, Rockefeller's words came back to haunt him as the Rockefeller name is forever associated with the infamous Ludlow Massacre. Ludlow was a mining camp in southern Colorado. On April 20, 1914, nineteen striking miners were killed when the Colorado National Guard opened fire on a mining camp. The dead included women and children.

Rockefeller made clear his disdain for unions when he visited Sunrise in 1915 and advised workers to "steer clear of agitators and not make any demands for a raise in wages." Rockefeller instead assured workers the company had their best interest in mind and that the company would decide raises. Rockefeller later softened his stance on worker organization by creating the Rockefeller Plan. Under the Plan, CF&I miners and steelworkers could advocate the terms and conditions of their employment, thus avoiding unionization and strikes. However, the Plan had drawbacks. More skilled workers approved of Rockefeller's Plan because they now had bargaining power. However, many junior employees didn't benefit from it.

CF&I towns operated as a type of welfare capitalism where the company managed the housing and beautification projects; built hospitals and schools; organized clubs such as the YMCA; and started Americanization programs

The tipple at Sunrise iron mine featured prominently in a want ad for laborers in the Japanese yearbook. *Wyoming State Archives.*

of immigrant workers. Sunrise also had a church managed by the CF&I's Sociological Department. In addition, the Sociological Department boosted morale, loyalty and company beliefs through a magazine called *Camp & Plant*, printed in English, German, Spanish, Italian and Slavic. During the 1908 recession, loyal employees protested when CF&I curbed its Sociological Department programs.[117]

OTHER WYOMING RAILROADS

There were also other railroads around Sunrise. Those railroads include the Northern Division of the Colorado and Wyoming Railway; the Colorado and Southern at Hartville Junction; the Burlington and Missouri River Railway; and the Chicago, Burlington and Quincy Railroad.

The Colorado and Southern employed an extra gang of thirty-five Japanese workers at Horse Creek when it extended its lines from Fort Collins, Colorado, to Cheyenne, bypassing Union Pacific for a more direct route to Denver and to CF&I smelters at Pueblo. Some Japanese also worked as section hands in Lingle and Torrington. CB&Q extended its Guernsey railway line from the iron mines at Sunrise to Frannie, a small town that straddled Big Horn and Park Counties, and to Worland, near Yellowstone National Park.

In Wheatland, Cheyenne and Northern Railway employed about seventy "little brown men." The *Wyoming Tribune* said Japanese section hands on the C&N Railway had "been quitting in twos and threes" because they did not like their foreman. The Japanese eventually went on strike, but railway officials induced them to return to work. Cheyenne and Northern officials hired forty Greeks and planned to hire men of other nationalities in case the Japanese went on strike again.[118]

Union Pacific; Chicago, Burlington and Quincy; the Chicago, Milwaukee and St. Paul Railroad; and the Northern Pacific Railroad all had lines leading into Yellowstone National Park. The two major Japanese labor contractors operating in northern Wyoming were the Oriental Trading Company and the Shinzaburo Ban Company. Oriental Trading Company also supplied Japanese railroad gangs in Montana, Idaho and North Dakota. The Shinzaburo Ban Company, with offices in Sheridan and Cheyenne, Wyoming; Pocatello, Idaho; Denver, Colorado; and Kobe, Japan, was the main source of Japanese laborers in Sheridan.

PART VII

JAPANESE IN AGRICULTURE AND LOYALTY

CHAPTER 31

ALIEN LAND LAWS

The Japanese laid down roots as railroads expanded into central and northwestern Wyoming. Shuichi Ujifusa was the first Japanese person to make his home in Wyoming's Bighorn Basin, in 1906. Ujifusa was born in Japan in 1881. He settled in San Francisco, California, before removing to Rairden, where he worked as a foreman for the Chicago, Burlington and Quincy Railroad. He also worked in nearby sugar beet fields to earn extra money. Shortly after, he quit the railroad and pursued farming full time[119] at a time when the United States tried to discourage Asian immigrants from settling permanently in U.S. states and territories by limiting their ability to own land and property.

Under Wyoming's Homestead Law, citizens of the United States, or those who had declared their intention to become such, were qualified to settle on, enter and acquire title to up to 160 acres by establishing and maintaining a residence and improving upon the land for five years. Land laws didn't openly discriminate against the Japanese but instead used the coded terminology "aliens ineligible for citizenship." In January 1913, a headline in the *Natrona County Tribune* said, "Jap [Ujifusa] Farmer Buys Additional Land." This headline suggests there were ways to navigate alien land laws. One way was to form a legitimate Japanese-owned corporation, and another was to purchase land in the name of a Japanese American child and hold that land in trust. California closed these loopholes in 1920. During World War II, Wyoming was one of three states to pass an alien land law. After the war, the restraint on Japanese landownership loosened. Still, the law remained in effect in Wyoming until the University of Cincinnati Law School Alien Land Law Project successfully lobbied the Wyoming legislature for its removal in 2001.

In 1951, Ujifusa discovered oil on his farm. Former executive director of Heart Mountain Dakota Russell, who wrote an excellent article about the Japanese pioneers of Big Horn Basin, said the discovery of oil ensured Ujifusa a comfortable life for his family and allowed him to give back to the Worland community that had become his home.[120]

CHAPTER 32

SHERIDAN: KN GARDENS

Sheridan is in the north-central part of Wyoming. The area was an important staging area during the Indian Wars, but Sheridan County opened to settlers after the U.S. Army forced the Lakota and Cheyenne tribes onto reservations. Soon after, the Burlington and Missouri Railroad laid tracks in the area, giving life to coal mine communities such as Dietz, Monarch and Acme and local farms such as the Japanese-owned KN Gardens.

Even though Japanese people couldn't own land in Wyoming, KN Gardens became a successful Japanese truck farming business in Sheridan. Truck farming was an operation that allowed farmers to ship their produce to market when a railroad wasn't nearby. KN Gardens was located three miles west of Sheridan on Rural Route 1, near Big Goose Creek. The fields were irrigated using a nearby canal system that distributed water into furrows next to growing crops. KN Gardens had five partners during its existence between 1906 and 1919. The principal partners were Kasaburo Okazaki, Jiro Kaiizumi, Gengoro Nishizaki and Jay Yamashita. The fifth man, Kichi Akagi, left the business shortly after it opened.

Kasaburo Okazaki was born in Japan's Okayama-ken Prefecture in 1881. He immigrated in 1905. Jiro Kaiizumi, also known as Jiro Kai, was a twenty-seven-year-old who also came in 1905. Before he settled in Sheridan, Kaiizumi worked in the sugar cane fields in Hawai'i. He was also a part-time apprentice photographer on Oahu. Jiro left Hawai'i for Wyoming, where he worked for the railroads until he lost the middle finger of his left hand.

Wyoming alien land laws prevented Japanese people from owning land. However, Jiro Kai(izumi), Kasaburo Okazaki, George Nishi(zaki) and Jay Yamashita owned KN Gardens. *Courtesy of Kathryn Mlsna.*

KN Gardens partners farmed twenty acres along Big Goose Creek. The State of Wyoming later purchased the land for a highway and irrigation channels. *Courtesy of Kathryn Mlsna.*

Gengoro Nishizaki was a twenty-two-year-old who immigrated in 1906. Kichi Akagi was a forty-five-year-old married man. He immigrated in 1901. Jay Yamashita came to Sheridan in 1907. He previously worked as a cook at a nearby horse farm before joining KN Gardens.

The partners leased two parcels of land. One parcel was twenty-five acres, and the other was five acres. The men treated the sandy loam soil with organic matter, furrowed the field, grew companion cover crops and covered the produce with translucent bags with pleats, a traditional Japanese technique that protects growing crops from sun and insect damage. This arduous process paid dividends when KN Gardens won first prizes for red onions, table squash and turnips at the Wyoming State Fair in Douglas in 1917.

KN Gardens closed after the State of Wyoming purchased the land to move forward on the construction of the Big Goose Creek canal project. The partners auctioned their livestock, farm equipment and household goods. In 2023 the Sheridan Community Land Trust, an organization dedicated to conservation, recreation and preserving Sheridan history, unveiled a Tongue River Water Trail plaque commemorating the former KN Gardens business and in recognition of the contribution of Japanese immigrants to Sheridan history.

After the sale, Kasaburo Okazaki married and adopted his wife's surname, Kimura. Together, they started a new business and grew a family. The couple had two sons, Kazuo and Tatsuru. Tatsuru is the father of Kathryn Mlsna, who shared family stories and photos of her grandfather's business ventures in Sheridan. Tatsuru said in an oral history on file with Densho that his father took the Kimura surname because he was adopted into his wife's family.[121] This tradition, known as *mukoyōshi*, preserves the name and occupation of the family when there is no suitable male heir.

The Kimuras purchased the Hotel Rex in downtown Sheridan after the previous owner was arrested for conducting an improper rooming house. The proprietor had her rooming house license revoked by the city council, and it was reissued to Kimura. The Rex Hotel was on Main Street on the second floor of Williams Hall. The hotel had a stained-glass canopied entrance and a handsome lobby with elegant chandeliers, easy chairs, desks and a long deep divan. A carpet layered over a soundproof layer of cork covered the lobby floors and corridors. In front of the lobby were four huge rooms that overlooked Main Street. One room had mahogany furniture, and the other rooms had oak. Two long hallways connected the remaining twenty-two rooms in the hotel. Each of these rooms had a skylight, oak

KN Gardens combined American dry farming and traditional Japanese techniques to grow award-winning produce. The translucent pleated bags prevented sun and insect damage. *Courtesy of Kathryn Mlsna.*

KN Gardens won first place for red onions, table squash and turnips at the Wyoming State Fair in Douglas in 1917. *Courtesy of Kathryn Mlsna.*

Kasaburo Okazaki operated the Hotel Rex after selling KN Gardens. He also married and adopted his wife's name, Kimura, in a practice called *mukoyōshi*. *Courtesy of Kathryn Mlsna.*

furniture, dull brass finished beds, the modern convenience of running hot and cold water and a radiator for steam heat.[122]

The Kimuras later sold the hotel and moved to Seattle to be closer to a larger Japanese community. Kasaburo died in Seattle in 1935, but his family continued to live in the city. Tatsuru, who now went by Eugene, and his older brother, Kazuo, both attended the University of Washington. On December 7, 1941, Eugene was at home working on his studies when he heard Japan had bombed Pearl Harbor. He couldn't believe it.

Nevertheless, he went to the University of Washington the next day. During President Roosevelt's "Day of Infamy" speech, some students sympathized with Eugene and his friends, while others let their racial prejudices come out. Other Asian groups tried to distinguish themselves from the Japanese by wearing buttons with their nationality to avoid being attacked. Finally, a dean at the University of Washington intervened on behalf of Kazuo and helped him transfer to Washington State University to continue his education. Kazuo later worked for a railroad in Montana.

The government detained Eugene and his mother at Camp Harmony, the unofficial euphemistic name given to a temporary incarceration center at the Puyallup Fairgrounds for 7,500 people of Japanese ancestry from western Washington and Alaska. The number of Japanese incarcerated under Executive Order 9066 almost equaled the population of nearby Puyallup. Eugene shared a room with his mother. It measured fifty square feet and had two beds with straw mattresses. The room had one window, and there was a single light bulb that hung from a single wire that stretched the entire length of the housing complex. The War Authority later transferred Camp Harmony's inmates to remote inland sites camps in Minidoka, Idaho; Tule Lake, California; and Heart Mountain, Wyoming.

Because some detainees were allowed to leave the compound for work, brothers Kazuo and Eugene started a letter campaign to Sheridan city officials asking for permission for Eugene and his mother to return to Sheridan. They said yes. Kasaburo's old partner George Nishizaki still lived in Sheridan and owned the Star Grocery. Eugene said, "George Nishi lived a very monastic life, and didn't know much about what was going on outside the store." When the Kimuras arrived, George suggested Eugene and his mother stay at the old family business at the Rex Hotel. Unfortunately, the Rex Hotel was no longer the same reputable hotel once advertised in *The Official Hotel Red Book and Directory*. As mother and son walked down the once familiar hallway, doors opened and flashily dressed women stepped out to greet them. Eugene thought, "Hey, these are not, what shall I say, cultivated women." The Kimuras quickly moved out and found temporary quarters with the help of a local family.

Although he was born in Sheridan, Eugene didn't remember much about the people because he was very young when the family left town. He said, however, that the citizens were indifferent to the fact that he and his mom were Japanese. Then, one day Eugene passed by some older women as he walked to George Nishi's store. They looked at him and said, "Hey, there goes that Indian boy again." The women had mistaken him for a Native American from one of the nearby reservations.

This comment made Eugene smile. He said to himself, "I am finally called a 'native' American."[123]

Kimura signed up for the draft after moving to Omaha, Nebraska, to attend the university. A draft board pronounced him 1-A, which meant Eugene had passed the army physical. He returned to the University of Nebraska and waited for his call to serve. Several months later, the army conducted a second physical. This time, the examining physician pressed hard on his appendectomy scar.

"Does that hurt?" he asked.

"Of course it hurts," replied Kimura.

"You're 4-F."

Kimura couldn't argue with the doctor or fight a system that didn't want him. So he took the train back to Nebraska and eventually earned a doctorate in pharmacology. Later in 1964, a subcommittee for the Judiciary House of Representatives admitted that many Japanese draft applicants were automatically disqualified based on race.[124]

Former KN Gardens partner Jiro Kai moved his family to Denver, Colorado, and lived in a predominantly Japanese area at 2014 Larimer Street. Jiro opened Kai Photography Studio and became the official photographer for the Denver School District. His granddaughter Aileen Tanimoto said Jiro traveled extensively throughout the western United States, documenting Japanese farmers and landscapes with his hand-cranked Kodak panoramic camera. His passion for photography earned him many awards, including a medal at the Paris Salon Photography Exhibition. Today, many of Jiro Kai's photographs are in the archives at the Denver Public Library.

Jiro met many famous people during his lifetime. The list included Ansel Adams, a photographer known for his black-and-white photography of western landscapes; acclaimed sculptor Isamu Noguchi; and Buffalo Bill Cody. By 1935, Jiro was tired of Colorado winters; he closed his studio, and the family moved to the more agreeable climate of Los Angeles, where he opened a photography studio and purchased real estate under his oldest son's name. After the Japanese bombed Pearl Harbor, the FBI arrested Jiro's wife, Mitsuko, and detained her for more than four months at the Terminal Island Federal Prison in Long Beach, but the government never told her immediate family. Her crime? She taught Japanese to Japanese American students. The FBI interrogated Mitsuko every four hours for more than a week. Then, without being charged with a crime, she was paroled to Poston I.

The Poston War Relocation Center was on a Native American reservation in Arizona. The War Relocation Authority and the Bureau of Indian Affairs jointly administered the center. There were three camps: Poston I, Poston II and Poston III. These camps were commonly called Roastin', Toastin' and Dustin', a reference to Arizona's brutally hot and dusty climate.

The FBI gave Tanimoto's mother, Sarah, and her aunt, uncle and grandfather Jiro one week to sell their possessions before their internment at Santa Anita Assembly Center. Santa Anita was a converted horse racing track. It had guards, barbed wire and searchlights, and the government

Post–KN Gardens photograph of Jiro Kai(izumi), baby Ruth, Mitsuko Kai, Kasaburo (Okazaki) Kimura, Jay Yamashita and George (Gengoro) Nishi(zaki). *Courtesy of Aileen Tanimoto.*

provided horse stalls as shelters. Still, the incarcerated provided their blankets and linens, toiletries, clothing, dishes and cookware and any personal belongings they could carry not written in Japanese. They later reunited with Mitsuko at Poston I. Despite the family's unfair treatment by the government, Aileen's uncle James Tsutomu Kai showed allegiance to America and enlisted in the army. He was joined by his younger brother after he graduated from high school.

Despite their unjust treatment, Jiro and Mitsuko remained loyal to their adopted country. After the war, Jiro took classes at night and passed the test to become an American citizen in the early 1950s. Mitsuko became a citizen in the 1970s.[125]

CHAPTER 33

QUESTIONS OF LOYALTY

The Japanese of Wyoming were loyal to their adopted state and country. They supported Red Cross subscription drives and purchased Liberty War Bonds. Many Japanese coal miners in Hanna contributed up to $10 for a Red Cross subscription drive for injured American service members during World War I.[126] A $10 donation in 1918 is equivalent to $200 in 2022.

In larger cities with Japanese associations, one out of five Japanese men gave to the Red Cross, and their wives became annual members. Japanese associations in several California cities; Nevada; Salt Lake City, Utah; and Colorado donated more than $3 million for the third Liberty Loan Drive.[127]

The Japanese registered for the draft during World War I, believing it was a pathway to citizenship. However, the U.S. Army inducted few Japanese volunteers because existing treaties gave them an exemption. The Japanese were also ineligible for citizenship because of the same tired rhetoric—the Japanese were unassimilable, and they did not legally fit the description of a "free white person."

Tom R. Yamamoto from Wyoming was just one of the five hundred Japanese granted citizenship for military service. Yamamoto was a cook at a ranch in Cokeville. He received his citizenship on March 7, 1921, at a ceremony in Kemmerer.[128] He trained at Fort Riley, Kansas, but he did not serve overseas. By 1952, the McCarran-Walter Immigration and Naturalization Act finally allowed Issei naturalization.

Heigoro Endo, a former Wyoming resident, became a citizen after World War II. He is the grandfather of Russell Endo, an accomplished author and retired professor of sociology and Asian American studies at the University of Colorado. Professor Endo said his grandfather worked as a teenager in Howell, Wyoming. After that, he moved to Utah and then to Terminal Island in Los Angeles Harbor. He married, worked on sardine boats and became part of a large Issei fishing community called Fish Harbor. Endo eventually bought a tuna boat and sold his catch to the Coast Fisheries Cannery. Later, he started a sportfishing business.

His success allowed him to buy a new home in the Barton Hills community of Los Angeles Harbor. On March 30, 1942, the army's Western Defense Command evicted the family under the authority of Civilian Exclusion Order 2. The Endo family had seven days to leave their custom-built home. The FBI arrested Heigoro Endo three days later. Professor Endo said the FBI searched his grandfather's home without a warrant and then backdated the presidential warrant when it was issued eight days later.

Authorities held Heigoro without pressing charges at the Tuna Canyon Detention Station. The Department of Justice bound Endo over for a hearing on April 24, 1942, and tried him in a kangaroo court. As with a typical kangaroo court, Heigoro Endo was presumed guilty and had no legal counsel.

An FBI special agent and the regional U.S. attorney asked him about donations to various Japanese organizations and his association with the Compton Gakuen, a school the FBI claimed was directly controlled by the Japanese government. In addition, they claimed his fishing boats were "radio-equipped" to communicate with enemy crafts, and the government accused him of monitoring U.S. Navy traffic in Los Angeles Harbor. The government even asked why Heigoro visited Japan to see his dying mother.

The court gave Endo a loyalty test:

"Who do you want to win the war?"

"The U.S."

"Would you let your sons fight for the United States?"

"Yes."

"Are you opposed to the Japanese attack on Pearl Harbor?"

"Yes."

The FBI claimed they confiscated contraband cameras, guns and a binocular while searching Heigoro's house. Endo, in defense, presented receipts from the San Pedro Police Department showing he complied with a government request months earlier. The FBI finally released Endo. A day later, the FBI admitted to an "inadvertent mistake" in their original report. Endo reunited with his family at the Santa Anita Assembly Center outside Los Angeles. In October, the family transferred to a War Relocation Authority concentration camp in Jerome, Arkansas.

At the war's end, Heigoro Endo was too old to regain his former economic status. He worked as an apartment manager for a large Japanese resettlement community in Chicago for several years, but the family eventually returned to warm and sunny Southern California. Heigoro and his wife applied for U.S. citizenship in 1947. Because of existing laws regarding the naturalization of the Issei, it took eight years for Endo and his wife to receive their citizenship.

In 1948, Heigoro Endo filed a claim to recoup wartime losses under the Evacuation Claims Act. Unfortunately, because of his arrest in 1942, he received only two-thirds of the dollar amount requested.[129] In 1988, President Ronald Reagan signed HR 442 providing for reparations for surviving internees. All eligible Japanese Americans received a redress payment of $20,000 beginning in 1990.

Shiro Kumagai from Sweetwater County was another Japanese alien registered for the draft during World War I. Stacie Kageyama, a distant niece of Shiro Kumagai, said there is an unconfirmed family story that Shiro was a Communist. Perhaps he was a Socialist. He was one of three brothers who worked in the coal mines in Sweetwater County, where the Socialist Party had a visible presence in Wyoming since 1902. The Socialist Party appealed to Wyoming coal miners because of its worker-first platform, which resulted in better pay, shorter workdays and a safer work environment. Shiro Kumagai was later involved in strikes against the coal company, and Kageyama said her uncle was forced to leave Rock Springs. No one in the family knows why he left because Shiro had a falling out with his brothers. Shiro later resurfaced during World War II at Tule Lake under a new name, Byron Akitsuki.[130]

Tule Lake was the largest of the War Relocation Authority's ten camps for people of Japanese ancestry. It had a peak population of 18,789. It also was the most turbulent camp. It became a segregation center in 1943 for "disloyal" Japanese Americans who answered "no" on a confusing loyalty questionnaire. Two questions on the loyalty questionnaire caused confusion. Question 27 asked Nisei men if they would serve in combat units. The question also asked women if they would join an organization such as the Women's Army Auxiliary Corps. Question 28 was the most confusing. It asked individuals if they would swear allegiance to the

United States and renounce the emperor of Japan. This question was confusing because immigration laws barred the Japanese from citizenship. Furthermore, the Japanese recognized the emperor's position but weren't loyal to him. Therefore, renouncing their Japanese citizenship would leave them without a country.

The camp was placed under martial law from November 1943 to January 1944 because of escalating protests and unrest. Many former incarcerates later renounced their American citizenship after their release from Tule; this meant the United States could deport them. In March 1944, *Life* magazine featured an article about life at Tule Lake. Byron Akitsuki was one of the incarcerates whose picture appeared in the magazine. The accompanying article said Akitsuki was the executive secretary of a committee meeting with WRA officials about camp problems. The California State University Japanese American Digitization Project scanned the full text of Akitsuki's diary, and in it, Akitsuki recorded the proceedings of the Japanese advisory council and the unrest in Block 21.

After three decades in the States, Don Aoki's great-grandparents, the Hirayamas and Hamadas, returned to Japan between 1936 and 1938, leaving their descendants in Sacramento. Nikichi died in 1942. Nikichi and Asa's grandson Bill was an ROTC cadet at Sacramento High, and he intended to join the army after high school. When the Americans bombed Kumamoto, Asa looked up at the planes overhead and wondered if her grandson was on board, dropping the bombs.

John Hatsuki Hamada once carried the Union Pacific Coal Mine payroll in Rock Springs as a teenager. He was now forty-four. He and his wife, Haruye, had eight children between ten months and nineteen years. Their ninth child, Charlotte, was born in Poston in October 1942. While at Poston, Aoki's mom, Jeanne, and her brother Bill were the only adult children, so they completed the loyalty questionnaire with their parents in February 1943.

In replying to question 27, "Are you willing to serve in the United States armed forces on combat duty, wherever ordered?" respondents could only answer "yes" or "no." Bill said yes, but only if his family could return to their Sacramento farm. The authorities told Bill he could not qualify his answer, and they considered his response equivalent to a "no." Anyone who answered "no" on any of the loyalty questions was branded as "disloyal" and sent to Tule Lake.

John, Haruye and Jeanne had initially answered "yes" to loyalty questions 27 and 28. However, they changed their answers to "no-no" so that the authorities would not divide their family. As a result, the government transferred the entire Hamada family to the Tule Lake Segregation Center.

Aoki said his father, Frank Aoki, became radicalized, and he joined a pro-Japanese group, Sokuji Kikoku Hoshi Dan, and demonstrated against the administration. He renounced his American citizenship, and the War Relocation Agency transferred Frank to the Department of Justice Santa Fe prison camp in 1945. The government deported Frank to Japan at the end of the war. Ironically, Frank found employment with the occupation forces as a translator and was assigned to construct an American air base in Hokkaido.

John and Haruye sold their Sacramento farm in December 1944. At the war's end, they returned to John's ancestral home in Kumamoto Prefecture. The children, however, wanted to be somewhere other than Japan because some of their classmates bullied them as foreigners because they were born in the United States. As a result, the Hamada children were often taunted with chants of "Yankee, go home!"[131]

CHAPTER 34

THE UNION PACIFIC DURING WORLD WAR II

The War Relocation Authority did not incarcerate Japanese people of Wyoming during World War II because Executive Order 9066 only authorized the forced removal of all Japanese living on the West Coast. However, the Union Pacific Railroad fired all Japanese nationals working in Wyoming, but any Japanese people who worked for the Union Pacific Coal Company kept their jobs. In a letter addressed to United States attorney general Francis Biddle, W.M. Jeffers, president of Union Pacific, shared his reasoning behind the firings. He stated that it was Union Pacific's policy to employ the Japanese until the company "had evidence that they were dangerous." In February 1941, Union Pacific dismissed seventy-five Japanese employees replacing a main switch at Howell, under the suspicion of sabotage. Train engine and shop personnel also complained about Japanese employees, and Jeffers received several angry letters immediately asking him to fire employees of Japanese ancestry from their positions. Jeffers said he "felt impelled to take immediate action."

Kikuji Kumagai was one of the Japanese fired by Union Pacific. He worked for the Union Pacific Railroad as a section foreman at Ridge, a small town six miles east of Medicine Bow. Union Pacific gave Kumagai and his family forty-eight hours to leave section housing, and the Carbon County sheriff confiscated his rifle and Kodak camera. A neighbor helped the family find a place to live in Medicine Bow, and the Kumagai children attended school there. Other sympathetic families gave Kikuji odd jobs. But unfortunately, he couldn't earn enough to support a family of six, and

Elsie (Kageyama), Rose, Johnny, Kikuji Kumagai, Tamai and Tom. Kikuji was a section foreman until the Japanese bombed Pearl Harbor. *Courtesy of Stacie Kageyama.*

the family moved to Salt Lake City, Utah, to be closer to Kikuji's older brother Hyoza.[132]

The Japanese who worked in Wyoming coal mining communities kept their jobs because they were "essential" to America's war effort. One Japanese coal miner, Tom Kawaguchi, even died supporting the war. Kawaguchi came to the United States around 1905 and worked as a coal miner for the Union Pacific Coal Company at Reliance. He died on November 15, 1945, while processing coal. Company officials believed he fell into a mixing conveyor and was dragged through the tipple to the mine run boom. He was survived by a brother, T. Uchikoshi, at Quealy.[133]

Another Japanese worker fired by Union Pacific was George Sunada. He is the son of Morijiro Sunada. Morijiro came to Wyoming in 1908. The senior Sunada worked in the coal mines at Superior and eventually became a foreman. He was also part of the first Japanese first aid team. Morijiro later opened a laundry in Superior before moving to Green River.

George Sunada was born in Green River in 1919. After high school, he joined the Union Pacific as a section laborer and worked in Peru, Wyoming, and the Green River railroad yards. He later transferred to the car department and worked in the roundhouse. After Union Pacific fired all its Japanese employees, George joined the army and was assigned to the all-volunteer Japanese 442nd Regimental Combat Team.

After the war, the government passed legislation under the Selective Service Act of 1948, reinstating veterans to their former jobs. However, the Selective Service Act didn't apply to men of Japanese ancestry who served. The all-Japanese army unit, the 442nd, was the most decorated army unit for its size and length of service in the history of the U.S. military. The 442nd earned 4,000 Purple Hearts, 4,000 Bronze Stars, 560 Silver Stars, 21 Medals of Honor and 7 Presidential Unit Citations. Private First Class George Sunada was a Bronze Star recipient.

After the war, two men from the Union Pacific approached George in Denver. They asked him to sign a document stating he would not sue the railroad for not being hired back. George said, "I didn't want to go back to the railroad anyway, so I signed it."[134]

CHAPTER 35

IN THE SHADOW
OF HEART MOUNTAIN

Although the Heart Mountain Incarceration Center did not include any Wyoming Japanese, there were some Washakie County farmers who suggested that Shuichi Ujifusa and family be sent to Heart Mountain and their land given to white residents. Attorney Charles Harkins and a larger group of locals supported the Ujifusas. "These people were born here, they're raised here, they've homesteaded here," Harkins told the antagonists. "You're the people that moved in here, you're the people trying to take the land away, I think it's time that you leave."[135]

Shuichi Ujifusa continued working the land. His day started at dawn with the milking of his cows. After he finished his chores, like clockwork, he drove more than seventy miles to Heart Mountain and arrived at the confinement center each day at 8:00 a.m.

Former Heart Mountain executive director Dakota Russell wrote in his article about Japanese pioneers of Big Horn Basin that the guards were so used to Shuichi's daily visits that they didn't even stop him at the gates because he had been a regular visitor since December 1942. During his visits, he gave sage advice to the prisoners, such as how to care for themselves in Wyoming's cold weather, how to avoid contracting Rocky Mountain spotted fever and what types of flowers and shrubs to plant in the confine's gardens.

When Shuichi left each day at 3:30 p.m. for the evening milking of the cows, the guards barely looked up; they just waved him out. Then, in the early summer of 1942, the War Relocation Authority established a general policy that allowed internees to help with the seasonal harvest. The Ujifusa family placed ads in the *Heart Mountain Sentinel* for farm laborers, cooks and housekeepers. Because the competition among the Heart Mountain prisoners was so great, Ujifusa could afford to be choosy about the help he hired.[136]

CHAPTER 36

NORTHERN COLORADO
BEET FIELDS

During the southern Wyoming coal miners' strike, Union Pacific freight traffic in the division decreased by 25 percent, and the coal mining community of Hanna lost five hundred Japanese workers to the beet fields in Colorado and Kansas.[137] Several more Japanese section men in the Laramie yards left the Union Pacific in 1908 for the beet fields in northern Colorado. Then, in 1909, nearly all the Japanese section men along the Sixth District of the Wyoming Division resigned[138] for better-paying jobs in the Colorado beet fields at wages between $3.00 and $3.50.

When the Japanese left the coal fields during the mining strike in 1908, Wyoming coal mine officials secretly traveled to northern Colorado "to induce the several hundred Japs who are busy in the beet fields to return to the mines." When Hyrum Timothy, the Greeley district superintendent of Great Western Sugar Company, heard about the mine owners' underhanded tactics, he saved the Colorado beet industry by collecting $500 from local beet farmers. He and a Japanese labor contractor drove to a section northwest of Greeley and visited the Japanese beet harvesters in the field; he asked them to stay on the job. All the Japanese beet harvesters promised to stay and harvest the beet crop, and because Hyrum Timothy believed them, he paid their wages in advance.[139]

By 1909, as many as 2,100 Japanese workers thinned, hoed and topped beets in northern Colorado. In comparison, 442 Japanese lived in southern Colorado beet communities and only 25 Japanese worked in the beet fields of western Colorado. Southern and western Colorado had smaller Japanese communities because these areas were less accepting of the Japanese. Naoichi Hokosana was the contractor who brought many Japanese workers to the beet fields of northern Colorado. He was one of Colorado and Wyoming's most prominent labor contractors. He came to Denver, Colorado, in 1893.

The Japanese worked the beet fields of northern Colorado during the Wyoming coal mine strike. Fourteen people shared this two-room house. *Author's collection.*

By 1898, he had opened a restaurant, and in 1903, he became a labor contractor. In 1903, there were only 300 Japanese working in the beet fields of northern Colorado.[140]

The production of Colorado beet sugar had increased by 4,000 percent since the turn of the twentieth century. By 1904, the sugar industry in Colorado was an estimated $8 million.[141] There were nine beet sugar factories in Colorado. Six were north of Denver in Longmont, Loveland, Greeley, Eaton, Windsor and Fort Collins. In 1905, the towns of Windsor, Eaton and Greeley employed 1,500 foreign laborers, mainly Russians and Japanese.

A report by the U.S. Department of Agriculture said the factory in Loveland was one of the largest in northern Colorado, with arranged contracts of fourteen thousand acres of sugar beets for the growing campaign in 1905. The sugar beet factory in Loveland was unique because its railroad was dedicated purely to sugar production. The railway in east Loveland spanned twenty miles. The sugar express had a rolling stock and the ability to traverse the beet fields, and it connected through its switching facilities with other roads.

The community of Fort Collins also had an advantage in the growing sugar beet industry. Fort Collins not only had a sugar beet processing factory but was also home to the Fort Collins Beet Growers' Association, the Colorado Agricultural College (later Colorado State University) and an experimental agricultural station.[142]

CHAPTER 37

WYOMING'S
SUGAR BEET INDUSTRY

The Eden Irrigation and Land Company hired a crew of eight Japanese and two Koreans to create a canal system to regulate the annual water flow into the Green River Basin and deliver water to local farmers and livestock growers. The canal system was especially beneficial to the sugar beet industry because sugar beets are a high-maintenance crop that requires a large and continuous water supply during the early growing season. The Hanover Canal System, an irrigation project in 1905, opened the Big Horn Basin to farming. The Arapaho and Shoshone tribes also ceded all the land north of the Wind River down to the mouth of the Popo Agie River and the southeast corner of the reservation to the State of Wyoming to encourage settlement and farming in the area.

Families with high hopes began pouring in to homestead the soon-to-be-irrigated land north of the river. There was even a colony of five Japanese workers growing sugar beets in Worland in June 1908. The *Grit* described the five workers as having no detriment to any community. The newspaper said that the Japanese are industrious, strictly attentive to their affairs and they contributed nothing to the city treasury as lawbreakers and all together make good citizens—save in naturalization.

One of the Japanese people who settled in Worland was Ike Terakawa. He was the proprietor of the Worland Hotel, and he had engaged in raising sugar beets in various states on the Pacific coast and Montana. He established an eighty-acre sugar beet farm in southern Worland. The town of Worland later partnered with the Wyoming Sugar Company and built a sugar beet processing factory in 1917 to meet the demand of a growing industry. Many Japanese were among the seasonal employees or "sugar tramps" hired. On the first day of production, Wyoming Sugar processed 260 tons of beets.

On the eastern side of Wyoming, some Japanese workers in the tiny town of Torrington engaged in growing sugar beets in 1922. Two Japanese farmers, Sam Opaski and K. Hikichi, rented the H.M. Springer section with the expectation of planting 140 acres of beets. Other Japanese residents attempted to grow beets on J.M. Springer's 120-acre spread. The *Torrington Telegram* also mentioned that T. Sakurai intended to grow 50 acres of alfalfa preparatory to planting beets.

NOTES

Part I

1. "Jap Bound Over," *Cheyenne Daily Leader*, June 19, 1902.
2. "Thinks Japs Will Invade," *Copper Mountain Miner*, January 31, 1908, 1.
3. "Summoned Home," *Wyoming Tribune*, October 28, 1904, 5.
4. "Six Jap Warriors," *Wyoming Semi-Weekly Tribune*, November 22, 1904, 3.
5. "Japs Are Coming," *Daily Boomerang*, April 30, 1900, 3.
6. "Don't Like Japs," *Cheyenne Daily Sun Leader*, April 2, 1900, 2.
7. "Japanese Spies Inspect Fort D.A. Russell," *Cheyenne Daily Leader*, February 26, 1908, 8.
8. "May Build to Laramie," *Laramie Republican*, May 28, 1908, 1.
9. "Yankee Spy," *Cheyenne Daily Leader*, March 6, 1908, 7.
10. "Japanese Spies Watch Maneuvers in Wyoming," *Cheyenne Daily Leader*, August 9, 1908, 1.
11. "Funeral of the Mikado," *Wyoming Tribune*, December 13, 1912, 5.
12. Interview with Hyoza (Harry) Kumagai by Paul Kato, Utah State Historical Society Japanese American Oral History Program, December 9, 1975.
13. "Japs in Riot in Big Horn Canyon," *Big Horn County Rustler*, April 1, 1910, 1.
14. "Japs for Section Work," *Carbon County Journal*, March 31, 1900, 1.
15. United States Census, 1910 and 1920, FamilySearch.
16. Interview with Japanese in Utah, University of Utah Marriott Library Oral History Collection, Sen Nishiyama, interview conducted by Sandra Fuller on March 2, 1985.
17. W. Jeet Lauck, "Occupation Hazard of Unskilled Employees on the Railroads," presentation to the United States Railway Labor Board, 1921.
18. Hiram Hisonori Kano, *A History of Japanese in Nebraska* (Crawford, NE: Cottonwood Press, 1984, 4–5), a personal narrative sponsored by the Scottsbluff Public Library.

19. F.W. Green, "Advantages in the Use of Japanese Track Labor," Roadmaster, Canadian Pacific, Kamloops, BC, *Railway Age Gazette*, 1912, 950.

20. J.A. Ottman, "Possibilities of the Japanese as Track Foremen," *Railway Age Gazette*, 1912, 950.

21. "Section Laborer an Interesting Man," *Laramie Boomerang*, July 9, 1904, 4.

Part II

22. *Railroad: The Wyoming Industrial Journal*, November 1899, 131.

23. *Wyoming Press*, December 5, 1903, 1.

24. "Japs Excited: Suspect a Conspiracy to Blow Them Up with Powder," *Laramie Boomerang*, June 14, 1900, 6.

25. Barbara Allen Bogart, "Evanston, Wyoming," WyoHistory.org, November 8, 2014.

26. *Wyoming Industrial Journal*, April 1, 1903, 256.

27. *The Railway and Engineering Review*, August 17, 1901, 547.

28. "Local Gossip," *Wyoming Press*, November 10, 1906, 8.

29. "Fossil, Oregon Short Line Depot," National Park Service National Register of Historic Places Registration Form, 2013, 12.

30. "Murder at Fossil," *Evanston Register*, August 26, 1893, 3.

31. "Runaway Coal Cars Kill Jap Aviator," *The Miner*, March 3, 1916.

32. "Kick on Workmen's Law," *Encampment Record*, March 16, 1916, 7.

33. "Japanese Celebration," *Kemmerer Camera*, November 17, 1915, 3.

34. *Kemmerer Camera*, November 5, 1908, 1.

35. "Success of a Japanese," *Cheyenne Daily Leader*, February 2, 1909.

36. *Kemmerer Camera*, April 17, 1918, 8.

37. "Notice of Incorporation," *Kemmerer Republican*, August 9, 1918, 3.

Part III

38. Chamois Andersen, "A History of Coal and Mining in Wyoming," Wyoming State Geological Society, wsgs.wyo.gov.

39. Kumagai interview.

40. Don Aoki, *Japanese Pioneers of Wyoming*, Wyoming International Film Festival, 2022, used with permission from Aoki, producer.

41. "Japs Jiu Jitsu Office," *Cheyenne Daily Leader*, March 23, 1909, 3.

42. Kumagai interview.

43. Aoki, *Japanese Pioneers of Wyoming*.

44. "Japanese Parade in Rock Springs," *Wyoming Tribune*, November 3, 1905.

45. "Sing Banzais," *Wyoming Tribune*, November 3, 1905, 5.

46. "Novel Strike," *Wyoming Tribune*, November 7, 1905, 5.

47. Kumagai interview.

48. Ibid.

49. George Okano, interview by Mark Junge, Wyoming State Archives Oral History, OH-2027, 6-23-90, Tape 1, Side A.

50. "Shut-Down Is Complete," *Cheyenne Daily Leader*, May 26, 1907, 1.

51. "Troubles for Wyoming," *The Indicator*, June 1, 1907, 1.

52. "Japanese Are Eligible," *Sheridan Post*, July 19, 1907, 4.

53. *Coal Age*, 1916, 853.

54. "First Annual Field Day," *Rock Springs Miner*, August 12, 1916, 2.

Part IV

55. "The Yellow Men Depart," *Rawlins Republican*, February 15, 1902, 1.

56. "Assaulted a Jap Laborer," *Rawlins Republican*, January 18, 1902, 1.

57. "Japs All Leave," *Cheyenne Leader*, February 14, 1902, 4.

58. "Railroads," *Wyoming Industrial Journal*, August 1903, 74.

59. "Jap Laborers Again," *Cheyenne Daily Leader*, December 9, 1903, 8.

60. "Japanese of Rawlins Will Celebrate Fourth," *Wyoming Tribune*, June 21, 1917, 7.

61. "No. 5 in the Ditch," *Saratoga Sun*, January 28, 1909, 1.

62. "Cause of the Dana Wreck," *Carbon County Journal*, February 6, 1909, 1.

63. Anna A. Maley, "One Wyoming Mining Town," *International Socialist Review* (n.d.): 20.

64. Ibid., 21.

Part V

65. "Trouble Over Japanese Laborers," *Rawlins Semi-Weekly Republican*, May 5, 1900, 6.

66. "On a Rampage," *Wyoming Tribune*, May 5, 1905, 4.

67. *Wyoming Tribune*, April 17, 1900, 4.

68. "Americans and Japs Clash," *Laramie Boomerang*, March 16, 1908.

69. "Union Pacific Lays Off Japs to Make Places for White Men," *Semi-Weekly Boomerang*, March 16, 1908.

70. "To Abandon Worn Main," *Laramie Republican*, November 21, 1908, 7.

71. "Fast Work on New Pipe Line," *Laramie Boomerang*, May 18, 1908, 1.

72. "New Pipeline Nears Completion," *Laramie Boomerang*, June 18, 1908, 1.

73. "Greeks Strike; Work Tied Up," *Laramie Boomerang*, July 11, 1907, 1.

74. "Two Engines Buried," *Centennial Post*, March 9, 1912, 2.

75. *The Railway and Engineering Review*, August 17, 1901, 549.

76. "Forest Fires Raging," *Grand Encampment Herald*, August 8, 1902, 1.

77. "Japanese for Woods," *Laramie Republican*, July 10, 1907, 1.

78. Paul G. Redington, Forest Inspector, and Earle H. Clapp, Forest Assistant, "A Working Plan for a Portion of the Douglas Creek Watershed in the Wyoming Division of the Medicine Bow Forest Reserve Wyoming," 89.

79. Ibid., 7.

80. "Stock Train On Fire," *Daily Boomerang*, August 16, 1900, 3.

81. General Laws, Memorials and Resolutions of the Territory of Wyoming: Intermarriage, Chapter 83, 1869.

82. "Three at One Time," *Laramie Republican*, March 3, 1909, 1.

83. "Mismated in Laramie," *Laramie Republican*, February 26, 1910, 5.

84. "Refuses to Marry Jap to a White Maiden," *Park County Enterprise*, February 8, 1911, 8.

85. "Jap Prevents Train Wreck," *Laramie Boomerang*, April 6, 1906, 4.

86. *Railway Journal*, 1898.

87. "Wyoming Governor Orders Cut in Saloon Hours as Patriotic Measure," *Union Signal*, January 10, 1918, 3.

88. "What Railroads Are Doing," *American Issue*, January 1912, 11.

89. "Resigns Position at Red Buttes," *Laramie Republican*, May 9, 1907, 1.

90. "Twenty Injured," *Wyoming Tribune*, June 28, 1906, 5.

91. "Tornado Blows Train from Track," *Laramie Weekly Boomerang*, October 22, 1908, 4.

92. "Six Die When Wind Hurls Car Over Fill," *Cheyenne Daily Leader*, October 21, 1908, 1.

93. Department of the Interior United States Geological Survey, *Guidebook of the Western United States* (Washington, D.C.: Government Printing Office, 1915, 44).

94. *Wyoming Industrial Journal*, March 1, 1908, 4.

95. "Will Hold Inquest," *Laramie Republican*, February 2, 1909, 2.

Part VI

96. "Japanese Arrive," *Wyoming Tribune*, March 2, 1905.

97. "Jap Army Here," *Wyoming Tribune*, April 26, 1905, 5.

98. "U.P. Double Track," *Pine Bluffs Post*, May 12, 1911, 4.

99. "A Raging Torrent Engulfs West and South Cheyenne," *Wyoming Tribune*, May 21, 1904, 1.

100. "Awful Flood," *Cheyenne Daily Leader*, May 21, 1904, 1.

101. "Jap War Here," *Wyoming Semi-Weekly Tribune*, April 7, 1904, 4.

102. "Will Go to Pen," *Wyoming Tribune*, July 19, 1904, 1.

103. *Wyoming Tribune*, August 12, 1910, 5.

104. "Died of Blood Poisoning," *Wyoming Tribune*, April 24, 1905, 4.

105. "Convert Japs," *Wyoming Semi-Weekly Tribune*, September 1, 1905, 2.

106. George H. Warfel, assistant to the general manager in charge of safety, "Keeping in the Front Rank in Safety Work," *Union Pacific Magazine*, 1931, 25.

107. "Jap Laborer Killed," *Wyoming Tribune*, January 25, 1907, 2.

108. "Death Was Accident," *Wyoming Tribune*, January 28, 1907.

109. "Borie Wreck Death List Reaches Nine," *Cheyenne Daily Leader*, November 12, 1908, 1.

110. "Were Brakes Inspected?" *Cheyenne Daily Leader*, November 15, 1908, 3.

111. "Japanese Murders His White Wife and Makes Mysterious Escape," *Tribune Stockman Farmer*, May 5, 1911, 1.

112. Hearings Before the Committee on Immigration and Naturalization, House of Representatives, Sixty-Seventh Congress, 1921.

113. "Americanization Is Being Taught," *Wyoming State Tribune*, October 25, 1921, 9.

114. "Club Women Plan 'Neighborhood Americanization,'" *Deaver Sentinel*, July 12, 1919, 5.

115. Proceedings of the Anti-Asiatic League, 1908, 8.

116. "Progressive Guernsey Section," *Wyoming Industrial Journal*, August 1, 1907, 3.

117. Sunrise Mine Historic District registration, National Register of Historic Places, July 2006.

118. "Japs on Strike," *Wyoming Tribune*, April 6, 1908, 5.

Part VII

119. Dakota Russell, Executive Director, Heart Mountain World War II Confinement Site, "Japanese American Pioneers of the Bighorn Basin."

120. Ibid.

121. Eugene Tatsuru Kimura, Densho Visual History Collection, December 5, 2008.

122. "Hotel Rex Is Opened to the Public Today," *Sheridan Enterprise*, July 11, 1913, 5.

123. Kimura.

124. Hearings Before Subcommittee No. 1 of the Committee on the Judiciary House of Representatives, Eighty-Eighth Congress, Second Session, Bills to Amend the Immigration and Nationality Act, 1964, 894.

125. E-mail interview with Aileen Tanimoto.

126. "Red Cross Honor Roll," *Rawlins Republican*, June 3, 1918.

127. "Sons of Nippon Support Red Cross," Japanese Immigration Hearings. Sixty-Sixth Congress, July 12–14, 1920, 789.

128. "Cokeville Jap Made United States Citizen in Court at Kemerer," *Laramie Republican*, March 7, 1921, 2.

129. E-mail interview with Russ Endo.

130. E-mail interview with Stacie Kageyama.

131. E-mail interview with Don Aoki.

132. E-mail interview with Stacie Kageyama.

133. "Vet Mine Worker Killed on Tipple," *Rock Springs Daily Rocket*, November 16, 1945.

134. Densho Digital Repository.

135. Russell, "Japanese American Pioneers."

136. Ibid.

137. "Miners' Strike Hurts Business," *Laramie Boomerang*, September 10, 1908, 1.

138. "Japs Leaving Road," *Laramie Republican*, May 21, 1909.

139. "After Japs," *Laramie Republican*, September 10, 1908, 1.

140. "Japs Quitting," *Wyoming Tribune*, October 1, 1906, 8.

141. "Wealth in Beet Crop," *Sheridan Post*, December 2, 1904, 3.

142. "Progress of the Beet-Sugar Industry of the United States in 1905," U.S. Department of Agriculture, Report No. 82, 51–53.

INDEX

ABOUT THE AUTHOR

Dan Lyon is Japanese American but doesn't have roots in Wyoming. He wrote this book to answer a friend's question about the Japanese community in Cheyenne. In his spare time, Dan gives historic presentations about F.E. Warren Air Force Base and volunteers his time at church and helping people research their Japanese roots in Wyoming on behalf of the Wyoming State Archives.

Visit us at
www.historypress.com
....